# Preventive Work with Families

The role of mainstream services

the **information** store

📞01603 773114
email: tis@ccn.ac.uk

The National Children's Bureau was established as a registered charity in 1963. Our purpose is to identify and to promote the interests of all children and young people and to improve their status in a diverse society.

We work closely with professionals and policy makers to improve the lives of all children but especially those affected by family instability, young children, children with special needs or disabilities and those suffering the effects of poverty and deprivation.

We collect and disseminate information about children and promote good practice in children's services through research, policy and practice development, publications, seminars, training and an extensive library and information service.

The Bureau works in partnership with Children in Wales and Children in Scotland.

Published by National Children's Bureau Enterprises, the trading company for the National Children's Bureau, Registered Charity number 258825.

ISBN 900990 08 3

Printed by Biddles Short Run Books

Typeset by Goodfellow and Egan, Cambridge

# Contents

# List of figures

# Acknowledgements

This report was originally commissioned by the Joseph Rowntree Foundation as a 'think piece' to inform the thinking of its Trustees as they planned their strategy for funding research and development projects. The Joseph Rowntree Foundation has subsequently provided funding to enable the report to be published. We are very grateful to the Foundation for its support and would like to thank, in particular, Barbara Ballard and Pat Kneen.

In undertaking this review of preventive work and mainstream services we have benefitted enormously from the interest and expertise of many colleagues here at the Bureau. Our thanks to all those who participated in our seminars and provided us with information. Our thanks also to Janine Gregory and Sabina Collier for secretarial assistance throughout the project and to staff in the Publications Department, especially Sarah Buzza.

Several colleagues representing a range of different interests – education, health, social services, academia, crime prevention, and children's rights – have been kind enough to read the report in draft to provide very helpful comments. Our thanks to David Cracknell, Nigel Parton, David Utting, Liz Wharfe, Moira Gibbs, Christine McGuire and Rachel Hodgkin.

**Ruth Sinclair**                                                    **March 1997**
**Barbara Hearn**
**Gillian Pugh**

# The authors

**Ruth Sinclair** is Director of Research at the National Children's Bureau. Her latest publications include: *Planning to Care – Regulation, procedure and practice under the Children Act* (with Roger Grimshaw), published by the National Children's Bureau (1997) and *Acting on Principle – An examination of race and ethnicity in social service provision to children and families* (with Ravinder Barn and Dione Ferdinand) published by BAAF.

**Barbara Hearn** is Practice Development Director at the National Children's Bureau. She is author of *Setting up Family Group Projects – A Practical Guide* published by Longman (1992) and *Child and Family Support and Protection* published by the National Children's Bureau (1994).

**Gillian Pugh** is Chief Executive of The Thomas Coram Foundation. She was formerly Director of the Early Childhood Unit at the National Children's Bureau and has published widely on early years services and on support and education for parents. Recent titles include: *Education and Training for Work in the Early Years*, published by the National Children's Bureau (1996); *Contemporary Issues in the Early Years*, published by Paul Chapman (second edition, 1996) and *Confident Parents, Confident Children* (with Erica De'Ath and Celia Smith), published by the National Children's Bureau (1994).

# 1. Introduction

## Introduction

The future well-being of our society rests upon the foundations that are laid through today's children. Securing a positive future requires an environment that empowers families and enables them to promote the welfare of their children. Such an environment – family-friendly and child-centred – would recognise that all families need support, and that some families need additional, specific supports. Creating this environment, through an appropriate balance of services that are accessible to everyone and those targeted at families with greatest needs, is a major challenge for central government and local agencies.

Determining this apportionment is an enormously complex task. It requires considerable understanding of the needs of children and families and how these might be addressed effectively through the provision of services. The complexities of this debate apply to all social interventions, and are well illustrated by the controversial conclusions of the Audit Commission on the role of the health visiting service (Audit Commission, 1994). While acknowledging both the lack of evidence on health visitors' effectiveness and that reductions in service could have serious repercussions for children and families, the report, nonetheless, recommended that apart from a first visit, preventive health visiting should no longer be universally available. Equally complex are the current debates within child welfare on the appropriate role of family support within child protection services (DH, 1994).

Are there more general lessons that can be learnt from such examples about the role of services in promoting the well-being of families? In particular what do we know about the contribution of mainstream services to preventive work with families? That is the question which this paper sets out to explore. More specifically the purpose of this paper is to:

- establish what is currently known, from research and service evaluation, about the contribution of mainstream services to preventive work with families;
- identify any obvious gaps in our knowledge or in the way in which knowledge has been disseminated or developed into practice;
- suggest from this, topic areas that could usefully be researched or where service or practice developments might be introduced and evaluated.

While the primary focus of this paper is research and development, this is only meaningful within a policy context. Here we do no more than set out some markers towards that policy agenda; hopefully these can be taken up, developed and activated elsewhere.

## The structure of the report

It soon becomes clear in undertaking an exercise such as this, that it is necessary to establish clear parameters. This is not only to make the project manageable, it is also to establish a common understanding of the conceptual framework. So the first task of this report is to establish those parameters. In Section 2 the meanings of the three key phrases are discussed – **the needs of families, preventive work** and **mainstream services**.

The outcome from this discourse will delineate the boundaries around the themes of Section 3 – a review of current knowledge of research and practice developments. Again structure for the discussion is important. Rather than explore all possible forms of preventive work where a contribution is or may be made by mainstream services, we have chosen four themes. These are:

- initiatives to support and enhance the parenting task;
- child health surveillance programmes;
- social service work with children;
- preventing 'anti-social' behaviour in adolescence.

These themes have been chosen for a number of reasons: they are all areas of high public concern; they are areas where we would expect mainstream services to play a preventive role and where the cost of failing to do so is expensive; and they are topics where the foundations of a research base have been laid.

From our exploration of these four areas we will then draw together in Section 4 evidence on effective models of service delivery and the attributes of services which contribute to successful outcomes. Recognising that all the needs of children and families are unlikely to be met by any single mainstream service or any one intervention in isolation, it will be particularly important to consider the coordination of service planning and delivery.

Thought needs to be given to the measures of effectiveness that have been or could be used in assessing the value of the contribution of these services. Some of the methodological complexities in assessing the effectiveness of preventive work and possible ways of addressing these are discussed briefly in Section 5.

The overview of existing knowledge will highlight significant gaps which will be taken forward in Section 6. This section will focus on the issues and topics that need to be addressed if these gaps are to be lessened. Some of these questions this raises will be answered best through a research programme; others through new developments in services that are systematically evaluated. This section concludes with a priority research and development agenda.

Finally, we turn to the policy dimension and indicate necessary areas of change if mainstream services are to enhance the contribution they currently make to supporting families and promoting their well-being.

# 2. Setting the parameters

Before we can examine the contribution of mainstream services to preventive work with families it is necessary to clarify the parameters of the discussion. In this section we define what we see as the needs of families, preventive work with families and mainstream services.

## The needs of children and their families

It can be taken as a general maxim that the purpose of preventive services is to promote the welfare of children and the well-being of their families (Gibbons, 1989). Before we can consider more specifically what this might mean in terms of effective interventions we need to understand something of the needs of children. Perhaps even before that we should clarify the way in which we are using the term 'family'. The Joseph Rowntree Foundation has defined family in the following way – 'dependent children and their principal adult carers -in most cases their parent(s) or step-parent(s)' (Utting, 1995). We find this definition useful but would also follow Utting in recognising the potentially crucial role played by wider family members, especially grandparents and siblings, and the relative neglect of this in literature.

The extensive knowledge base on the development of children provides a general consensus on the needs of children. Here we use the work of Kellmer Pringle (1975), Cooper (1985) and others to identify what those elemental needs might be:

- basic physical care;
- affection;
- security;
- a sense of identity;
- stimulation;

- guidance and control;
- growing responsibility;
- a developing independence.

This broad-brush classification of the needs of children must be applied with an understanding of three further considerations.

First, the specific needs of children and young people within these broad groupings, change as children age – as will the requirements of parents in meeting the needs of their children at different ages and stages.

Second, each child is unique and so is his or her family situation. The interrelationship between a child's nature and the nurturing he or she receives influences his or her ultimate well-being. A generalised understanding of the needs of children and their families must not conflate the very particular needs of each child and family at a point in time.

Third, children's needs will be defined, in part, by society. So a child's needs must be understood within his or her particular context and culture (Woodhead, 1996).

In addressing the needs listed above, the starting point for most children is the family environment. Hence the needs of children are more likely to be met where families are enabled and supported in their parental task. To support the parent is to support the child.

There is no clear evidence that the needs of children are more likely to be met by families of a particular structure or type. What is more important is the nature and quality of parenting (Schaffer, 1990; Richards, 1994).

There is growing research knowledge about different styles of parenting and the impact that these have on outcomes for children (Patterson, 1982; Butler, 1985; Wilson, 1987; West and Farrington, 1982; Shucksmith, and others, 1995; Pugh and others, 1994). Some of these have identified positive and negative qualities within parental/child relationships and are summarised in Figure 1 on page 6.

Positive, nurturing relationships between children and parent(s) are a crucial foundation for well adjusted development in children. The capacity of parents to offer this depends on wider environmental factors – on adequate income and housing, good health, family-friendly employment policies, the availability of day care and other support services.

As Leach has commented,

However solidly these relationships are founded, they alone cannot ensure that children's needs are met because even the most loving and privileged of parents can only do what society arranges, allows and supports. (Leach, 1993)

| Figure I   Positive and negative qualities in parenting | |
| --- | --- |
| *positive* | *negative* |
| authoritative | authoritarian, permissive |
| warm and affectionate | cold and hostile |
| clear limit setting | inconsistent rules |
| quick to recognise needs | unresponsive to needs |
| accepting of faults | rejecting |
| predictable and consistent | unpredictable |
| respecting the individual | disrespectful |
| open and effective communication | inadequate supervision |
| recognising good qualities/ behaviour | punishing bad qualities/behaviour |
| empathic | inappropriate expectations |

There is mounting evidence about the failure of our society to adequately address the needs of children, to ensure the 'permitting circumstances' which underpin parents' ability to provide good enough parenting. Research points to the increasing numbers of children living in poverty and with inadequate housing (Bradshaw, 1990; Kempson, 1996) and the consequences of that in terms of children's health, development and educational achievement (Kumar, 1993; Oppenheim and Harper, 1996).

It is unsurprising that overviews of preventive work continue to recognise the importance of these wider social and economic agendas, for instance in acknowledging the deep-seated structural influences on the health of children, Bryant (1986) concludes:

Health surveillance on its own may have little effect unless it is accompanied by measures to relieve poverty, poor housing and other environmental stress.

In this report we have purposefully chosen to focus on the needs of children rather than their problems. This enables the concept of prevention to be defined in an affirmative way. Thus we can enlarge on our earlier statement and define prevention as – 'the promotion of child welfare by enabling children and young people

**Figure 2 Journey through childhood: building supports and using preventive services to minimise the hazards**

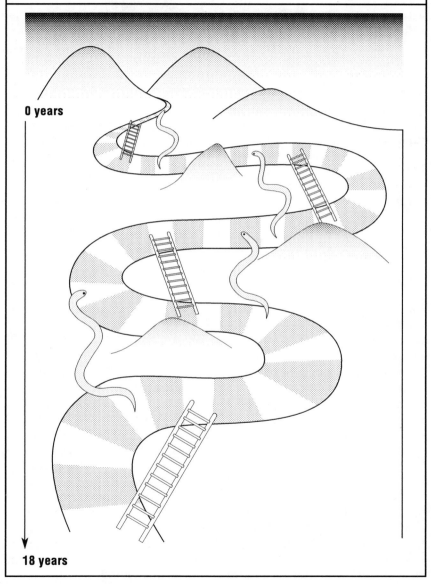

0 years

18 years

© National Children's Bureau

to develop to their full potential, and the promotion of family well-being by enabling parents/carers to meet the overall needs of their children and themselves'.

The ultimate aim must be to see as many young people as possible reach adulthood as self-sufficient, confident, socially responsible individuals. The passage through childhood, from birth to 18 years, can be pictured as a journey, but possibly a journey through territory that is akin to a *Snakes and Ladders* board; the *Ladders* representing positive supports and enablers while the Snakes are the mishaps, mistreatment, and miseries along the way. Of course the terrain of every child's board will be different; some will start from lush plains, others from rocky hills; some may be handicapped by burdens, others may acquire unnecessary baggage along the way.

The contribution of preventive services is to provide more *Ladders* and remove or minimise the *Snakes* and their impact; to ensure that the baggage carried contains sustenance rather than weights. In themselves preventive services can only have a limited impact on the uneven terrain. This is likely to require new macro social economic policies aimed at ensuring adequate income and housing standards for all families.

## Preventive work: what does it mean?

The concept of preventive work is well established as a particular approach to addressing problems and often occurs as a division within mainstream services: preventive medicine; preventive social work; diversion from crime; preventive work with families. There is also a general or broad understanding of what is meant by preventive work, perhaps best encapsulated by the phrase 'better a fence at the top of a cliff than an ambulance at the bottom'.

At an elementary level this is expressing the notion that simple, relatively inexpensive measures, put into effect early, can save the need for more complex interventions later – and in the process the person receiving the service will be spared much future agony. Certainly this is true if there is a known and direct relationship between the solution and the problem it is trying to prevent – if, in fact, the fences do prevent people from crashing to the foot of the cliff. But what if placing a fence on the cliff means that the person who wishes to 'fall over' now consumes a bottle of paracetamol and the ambulances are still needed? In this case the preventive measures are not effective; for those people determined to 'fall' they did not identify accurately what was to be prevented.

In looking more closely at the concept of prevention it has been suggested that the term can have no meaning unless and until there is clarity about 'what' is being prevented.

> The difficulty with the use of the term 'prevention'...lies not so much in the intrinsic meaning of the word as in the differences of meaning that arise once an object is placed after the verb...to prevent WHAT? (Hardiker and others, 1991a, p43)

The list of problems which mainstream services are currently trying to prevent is large and diverse. In terms of specific outcomes this might include family breakdown, poor health, developmental delay, child accidents, child abuse, low educational attainment, truancy or exclusion from school, juvenile offending, mental health problems including suicidal behaviours in young people, substance misuse, early unwanted pregnancy.

Even where there is a clear idea of what is to be prevented, before any programme or intervention can be planned to address that, it is very necessary to have a full understanding of the characteristics of the phenomenon, any associated risk or protective factors that may have an impact on it – recognising the likely plurality of casual links. For instance, in aiming to reduce the level of teenage pregnancies it is important to know the extent to which such pregnancies are unwanted, and where this is the case whether conception is due to lack of sex education, poor availability of contraception, or the lack of confidence to be assertive in the 'heat of the moment'. Preventive programmes devised without such knowledge are much less likely to be effective.

Similarly the need to build preventive strategies around a sound knowledge of risk factors is at the heart of the current controversy over the strategy for preventing the spread of AIDS. Those who believe there was a misrepresentation, deliberate or otherwise, of the risks to the general population from the HIV virus suggest that the chosen prevention strategy, which targeted the total population, was unnecessarily expensive, diverted resources from real need, had an unnecessary and harmful impact on many in the population, and did not target adequately those at greatest risk. Moreover this example illustrates the importance of recognising the political dimension in our understanding of prevention (Freeman, 1992), and of understanding the potential for unintended consequences which must be managed.

Identifying risk factors is not always easy. As Farrington has pointed out in respect of preventing youth crime, identifying which risk factors are causal and which merely predictive or symptomatic is problematic; furthermore most risk factors tend to coincide and be interrelated (Farrington, 1996). Further controversies arise when we move beyond predicting probabilities of particular social behaviours within population groups to attempting to identify individuals at risk (Parton, 1985).

The identification of risk and protective factors must be seen in terms of probabilities; in the field of human behaviours these cannot be regarded as an absolute, nor as predictive. In this way intervention at an early stage can be viewed as shifting the balance of future probability, of changing the distribution between good and bad outcomes to optimise the good and minimise the bad.

Nonetheless development of knowledge of risk and protective factors has to be seen as the key to developing effective preventive strategies.

## Levels of prevention

It is clear that the concept of prevention cannot imply a once-only intervention. If we have failed in preventing the fall from the cliff, we still send the ambulance in an effort to prevent unnecessary further harm. If this is also referred to as 'preventive work' then we need to distinguish the one from the other. Thus the concept of prevention needs to be understood in terms of the level of the preventive intervention.

There have been many schema for describing these levels, mostly based on the accepted division in medical interventions into primary, secondary and tertiary prevention. This trilogy is not without its criticisms, but nonetheless provides a useful framework (Coohey and Marsh, 1995). The concept of the level of prevention focuses on the stage of problem formation. This in turn suggests an appropriate target population for effective intervention. Expressed simply, primary prevention relates to a stage before problems have manifest and are best targeted at whole populations; in health care terms this could mean a programme to prevent the onset of disease through ensuring the whole population has access to clean water, or to immunisation.

Secondary prevention implies that a problem has already become apparent and action is needed to prevent this becoming more serious or deep-seated. In the field of crime this can be illustrated by interventions to prevent young people who have committed their first minor crime from re-offending and is likely to be targeted at these young people as a group. In education this may refer to additional input when delayed language development has been identified.

Where problems are multiple, complex or long-standing positive change will require intervention which is focused on the particular circumstances of the individual. This is tertiary level prevention. In social work this could be highly focused, in-depth work with a child on the Child Protection Register to prevent the need to remove the child from the family.

Hardiker in her discussion on prevention in social welfare also employs quaternary prevention – work to reduce the impact of an intrusive intervention, for instance the impact on a child who is likely to remain in the care of the local authority (Hardiker and others, 1991a). In terms of education, an example may be work to minimise the impact on the child of exclusion from school.

Having illustrated these four levels of preventive work, it is apparent that this has incorporated a wide range of work with families. Does this then mean that the concept 'preventive work' has become so broad that it has lost its meaning? The confusions and misunderstandings that arise from this conceptualisation has led others to suggest alternatives – such as prevention, treatment and rehabilitation (Coohey and Marsh, 1995) or prevention, intervention, and postvention, as favoured in respect of suicide (Dunne-Maxim, 1992). Another approach is to differentiate more clearly the characteristics of these three levels.

*Characteristics of preventive work at different levels*
So far we have suggested that levels of prevention can be distinguished by the stage of problem formation and the appropriate target. Hardiker and colleagues take this further and illustrate how aspects of preventive work in child welfare vary along a total of six key dimensions: practice ideology; stage of problem development; major unit of need; principal targets for intervention; objectives of intervention; dominant mode of practice. Figure 3 below identifies these key characteristics for three levels of prevention. This relates specifically to social services interventions in child welfare but the concepts are transferable to other service interventions.

Charting the characteristics of interventions in this way may present a conceptual neatness that is rarely reflected in reality.

## Figure 3    Key characteristics and levels of prevention

| *Levels of prevention* | *Primary* |
| --- | --- |
| *Key characteristics* | |
| 1. Practice ideology | • development<br>• change systems rather than people<br>• empowerment |
| 2. Stage of problem development (assessment of risk and/ or need) | • low or containable risk<br>• problems common to many (vulnerable groups)<br>• citizens rather than clients |
| 3. Major unit of need | • localities<br>• vulnerable groups |
| 4. Principal targets for intervention | • welfare institutions<br>• community networks<br>• social policy |
| 5. Objectives of intervention | • reallocation of resources<br>• redistribution of power/control over resources (incl. resources of s/w agencies)<br>• increased rights for disadvantaged groups |
| 6. Dominant mode of practice | • community action<br>• community development<br>• community social work |

**Source:** *Policies and Practices in Preventive Child Care* (1991a)
Hardiker, P., Exton, K., Barker, M.

| Secondary | Tertiary |
|---|---|
| • welfare<br>• help for the client<br>• assessments of need | • judicial<br>• rescue the victim<br>• punish the villain |
| • low/medium risk but high perceived need<br>• acute crisis or early stage of problem<br>• short-term client | • Chronic, well established problems<br>• high risk of harm to self or others<br>• high need for protection of child<br>• perceptions of parental need may be low |
| • nuclear family | • individual family member(s) perceived as problematic or in need of rescue/protection |
| • family systems<br>• support networks<br>• welfare institutions | • personal change |
| • enhanced family functioning<br>• enhanced support networks<br>• family's increased awareness, and motivation to make use of existing resources<br>• welfare institutions more responsible to people's needs | • better adjusted, less deviant individuals<br>• self-supporting families |
| • generic, multi-role practitioner<br>• social care planning<br>• social casework | • individual casework<br>• treatment/therapy |

There are many services which overlap these levels of prevention and many users whose needs must be reflected at several points on these continua (Fuller, 1987). Similarly preventive work is deeply rooted in both values and policies (Hardiker and others, 1991b). Nonetheless delineating preventive work in this way is a useful starting point from which to examine specifically the role of mainstream services.

A further dimension could be added to this chart, namely the nature of the service provision. Are there characteristics of service provision which are more likely to be associated with one level of prevention than with others, such as mainstream or specialist; services which are open access or which require a professional referral; services which are state funded or privately purchased? We return to this later.

This cross over between the severity of a problem, the appropriate level of intervention and the nature of the services is well illustrated by the accepted concept of tiers in mental health services. This model has been depicted in some detail in several key documents on child and adolescent mental health services (DH and DoE, 1995; NHS/HAS, 1995; Kurtz, 1996). Figure 4 presents a summarised version of a tiered model of child and adolescent mental health services. Similar concepts are reflected in the five stages in the identification and assessment of pupils with Special Educational Needs (see Figure 5). As both these models reflect service delivery they do not include primary promotion, such as health promotion.

The relationship between the nature of the service and its role in prevention is an important focus for this report. We shall return to this later, following our exploration of 'mainstream services' in the next section.

## Levels of prevention and appropriate intervention

Depicting preventive work in this way, provides a framework for developing effective interventions. Again there is much evidence of failed interventions where there is a mis-match between key characteristics and the level of prevention.

For instance evidence of the limited impact of much social work intervention in the 1960s and 1970s, where on-going, unfocused support was offered even though the stage of problem formation suggested the need for interventions that were at least secondary and probably at the tertiary prevention level (Fischer, 1973;

## Figure 4 A tiered model of child and adolescent mental health services

A comprehensive child mental health service will operate at several levels or tiers to meet the needs of the local population:

**Level 1** Problems that require additional professional help at the primary care level for example, teachers and field social workers.

**Level 2** More serious problems that require the intervention of professionals with specialist knowledge of child mental health for example community and hospital paediatrician, specially trained social workers and others. These individuals provide a unprofessional service and operate as a network rather than as a core team.

**Level 3** Serious and complex disorders that require the specialist help of a multi-professional core team. Core members of the child mental health team include child psychiatrists, child psychologists, child and community mental health nurses, specialist social workers, teachers, psychotherapists, family therapists and other specialist therapists.

**Level 4** Extremely severe and complex problems that have failed to respond to help at the other levels. Very specialist day patient and residential/inpatient care facilities are required for this level of disorder.

**Source:** *A Comprehensive Child and Adolescent Mental Health Service* Pearce and Holmes, 1994

## Figure 5 Stages in the identification and assessment of Special Educational Needs

**Stage 1** Class or subject teachers identify or register a child's special educational needs and, consulting the school's SEN coordinator, take initial action

**Stage 2** The school's SEN coordinator takes lead responsibility for gathering information and for coordinating the child's special educational provision, working with the child's teachers

**Stage 3** Teachers and the SEN coordinator are supported by specialists from outside the school

**Stage 4** The LEA considers the need for a statutory assessment and, if appropriate, make a multidisciplinary assessment

**Stage 5** The LEA considers the need for a statement of special educational needs and, if appropriate, make a statement and arrange, monitor and review provision.

**Source:** *Identification and Assessment of Special Educational Needs: Code of Practice*, 1995

1976). Other evaluations of social work practice pointed to the effectiveness of interventions that were time limited, intensive and focused on specific, identified problem behaviours or relationships (Reid and Hanrahan, 1980; Sheldon, 1986; Stein and Gambrill, 1977). Here the families in receipt of services had already acquired client status and therefore third level preventive services were appropriate.

Services which focus on primary interventions are likely to be less intensive but spread more widely. But even primary level interventions have to have sufficient impetus if they are to effect change. This has been well illustrated with the analogy of a boiling pot – if you do just enough to make the pot simmer but it never boils then no change occurs; sufficient inputs of energy are needed to bring things to the boil – to effect change – after that only small inputs are needed to keep things simmering (see Slavin, 1992, reviewing the effects of programmes to prevent school failure). Similarly outcome and cost-effectiveness studies are necessary to indicate where over-elaborate primary preventions are unnecessary and indeed may be counterproductive, for instance concerns about physical effects from child development screening (Butler, 1989).

Progression through the levels of prevention also increases the intrusiveness of the intervention and therefore impacts on the degree of control retained by the child or family. There is growing evidence that working in partnership and involving users is not only more respectful, it is also more effective, whether this is with young people themselves or their parents (see for example Gardner, 1982; Woodhead, 1985; Pugh and De'Ath, 1989; Nuffield Health Unit, 1996; Willow, 1996).

Undoubtedly thinking about the particular level of prevention helps to clarify options for intervention. However, such theoretical constructs must be used flexibly, recognising for instance that problems are often multi-faceted and that more than one level of intervention may be required at any one time. Much of the literature in the crime prevention field points to the need for a variety of approaches to be adopted simultaneously. In examining ways in which child-rearing can be improved and hence prevent delinquency, Crime Concern suggest a multi-level approach which combines universal services available to all families; neighbourhood services targeted at particular areas with a high prevalence of the particular problem – in this case crime; and family preservation services for families most at risk (Utting and others, 1993).

Similar models have been explored, but not yet evaluated, in respect of family support or in the coordination of community child health and social services (Hearn, 1995; Audit Commission, 1994; Rea Price and Pugh, 1995). Again, we will return to consider multi-level, multi-functional services later in this report.

The purpose of this section has been to consider what is meant by the term 'preventive work' The trilogy of primary, secondary and tertiary prevention was used to explore some of the dimensions of preventive work. This points to several factors which will influence the effectiveness of preventive interventions: clarity about the objectives of the intervention; an understanding of the risk and protective factors – the points of leverage for effecting change; ensuring a level of prevention appropriate to the state of the problem and applied with sufficient momentum; involving children and families in the preventive work. We have also suggested that defining preventive work is not without controversy, particularly in terms of its political dimension and practical application.

Some of the methodological issues in evaluating the effectiveness of preventive interventions are addressed in a later section. We turn now to the third theme in our title, mainstream services, and seek a suitable definition.

## Mainstream services

Although the term 'mainstream services' probably has a shared meaning in a common sense, everyday sort of way, when one tries to define it, the concept immediately becomes more complex. One could think of it in the terms used by the Joseph Rowntree Foundation in respect of its programme for promoting successful parenting and preventing problems developing in the family – that is health, education, social services, the judicial system and the police (see Utting, 1995). But would we deem all the services provided by these agencies to be mainstream, including the most specialist? So are there any criteria which would help in clarifying what might be termed 'mainstream'?

While such distinctions may appear to be an intellectual exercise conducted for the purposes of this project, we believe they are a necessary pre-requisite to understanding the role of mainstream services in effective preventive work. So in this section we examine possible criteria for defining mainstream services and how these might apply to particular services; we relate this to the levels of prevention, as discussed earlier; and from this set the parameters for later considering the contribution of mainstream services to preventive work.

## Defining 'mainstream' services

Support services can be described along several dimensions. While some of these dimensions may be related, they are as likely to be independent, with no one common pattern which binds them together. Here we look at the dimensions separately, but recognise the complex interweaving which relates one to the other.

Some of these dimensions, taken alone, can act as a criterion for determining whether a service is mainstream or not. Some may be necessary but not sufficient criteria. Determining whether any particular service is not mainstream depends upon a particular mix of these features.

**Universality:** there are only a limited number of services to families which are universal in the sense that they are available to almost everyone; the most important are schooling for five-to 16-year-olds; primary health care through a general practice; child benefit in respect of children under 17 or still in education; and community police services. All these services must be regarded as mainstream.

**Open access:** *open access services* are those that are available to anyone who presents themselves. By definition universal services are open access, but open access service will not necessarily be universal; they may not be available to everyone in a community or to every community. For instance, play and leisure services such as a youth club may be open to those who wish to attend, but many young people will not have that opportunity. Similarly some services will be open access within their locality but will be targeted at particular areas and are not available universally. Some services which appear open access, may be regarded as restricted or specialist – for instance the activities of churches or other faith communities may not be acceptable to non-believers. Given these limitations, such services will not be mainstream. Media services are open access; some like TV can also be regarded as universal. The very openess of access and hence the limited ability to target is a significant factor in the effectiveness of services such as the media in playing a preventive role.

**Referral process:** another dimension is the process for referral. Open access is one form of referral. This might be by *self-referral* by way of advice or exchange of information. For instance where a health visitor suggests to a parent that he/she will find a parent education class useful and facilitates attendance, this still allows direct access by the user and can be considered open access. Other self-referral services may require a form of assessment before the referral is accepted, for instance access to a Home-Start volunteer, or the payment of income support. This can be called *filtered access.*

Where access to a service, such as a hospital consultant or a family therapist, can only be gained by referral from another professional this is *restricted or referred access.* Similarly, help from a social services duty desk is an open access service, but not so a respite care service.

While open-access and possibly filtered access services may be regarded as mainstream, it is unlikely that any referred access service can be considered mainstream.

At times people may be the unwilling subject of referral. This is often the case in respect of the child protection and criminal justice systems. This would seem to eliminate these services from the category of mainstream. Furthermore the negative connotations of such services and their agency as a whole may well impact upon a family's willingness to self-refer even when a lower level of preventive work may still have been effective.

**Specialist/targeted services:** closely linked to the referral process is the extent to which services are regarded as *specialist* and *targeted* at specific individuals or groups. Some specialist services may be accessed by self-referral, especially in the private sector, for instance psychiatric services, but most in the state sector will require contact through a professional. These are likely to be tertiary or fourth level preventive services and not within the definition of mainstream.

**Cost to user:** should we restrict our definition of mainstream services to those that are either free to the user, or which are subject to a means test? This would certainly include the universal services and many of the front line services of other agencies. However it would exclude childminders, one of the most commonly used and readily accessible services for families with younger children. However childminding paid for or subsidised by social services on the basis of assessed need would fulfil this criteria but not that of self-referral, highlighting the complex interweave of these criteria. A reasonable clarification is to include as mainstream those services which may be purchased, but which are also made available to those unable to pay.

**Source of funding:** regardless of who provides a service, is *the funder* an appropriate criterion by which to judge a service as mainstream? Certainly in times past the funding of a service from the public purse would have lent weight to its inclusion as 'mainstream'. With the shrinking of public provision this is less likely, as exemplified by council house provision. We concluded that public funding is an important additional attribute when considering if a service is mainstream.

**Provider sectors:** services to families, at all levels of prevention, may be provided by either *statutory agencies, the voluntary, not-for-profit or the private sector*. There is no simple relationship between the previously discussed dimensions and the status of the provider. All sectors may or may not charge the user directly for services; all may provide open access services; all operate at several levels in the preventive framework. This dimension, on its own, therefore is unlikely to determine whether a service is mainstream.

**Regulation or inspection of services:** with changed patterns of public funding and service delivery, central and local government have enhanced their roles as regulator or inspector of services. There are some minimum standards applicable to all services such as health and safety, race relations and sex discrimination; others will be subject to additional, specific regulation and inspection. Only those services subject to such inspection and regulation can be regarded as mainstream. Hence a counselling service like Relate which may fit other criteria cannot be considered mainstream.

**The level of prevention:** in the previous section we considered the key characteristics of preventive services, drawing on the work of Hardiker and colleagues. We would now add a seventh dimension to Figure 3 on page 12, highlighting the nature of services likely to be appropriate at different levels of prevention.

**Figure 3a   The seventh characteristic**

| Seventh characteristic | Primary prevention | Secondary prevention | Tertiary prevention |
| --- | --- | --- | --- |
| Nature of service | • universal<br>• open-access<br>• generalist/multi-disciplinary skills | • self-selected<br>• filtered access<br>• generalist within a profession | • selected clients<br>• referred access<br>• specialist within a profession |

Pulling this discussion together, it is possible to offer a definition of mainstream services. Such a definition comes in three parts: those services which are definitely mainstream; those which may be mainstream because they have some but not necessarily all the qualifying criteria; those services which are definitely not mainstream. This is explained in more detail in Figure 6 below.

These deliberations on the concepts of prevention and mainstream have served two purposes. By clarifying key characteristics of services it provides a much firmer understanding on which to develop proposals for effective preventive services and, it has established the focus for the rest of this report. It is time now to relate this conceptual thinking to more concrete evidence of the needs of families, their experience of the services available and evaluations of their effectiveness in preventing needs amplifying.

---

**Figure 6    A definition of mainstream services**

**Mainstream:** services with **all** the following characteristics:

- universally available;
- open access or accessed through self-referral and an assessment process;
- free or means tested;
- publicly funded;
- subject to statutory regulation and inspection;
- primary or possibly secondary level prevention services.

**Possibly mainstream:** services with **some, but not necessarily all** the above characteristics.

**Not mainstream:** services with any of the following characteristic:

- can only be accessed by referral;
- specialist;
- not subject to statutory regulation and inspection;
- operating at tertiary or fourth level of prevention.

---

# 3. Aspects of preventive work with families

## The contribution of mainstream services

Having considered the needs of families and spent some time refining the concepts of preventive work and mainstream services these are now brought together in a review of knowledge about the contribution of such services to promoting the welfare of children and their families. What mainstream services are currently being offered to families and when? What attributes of these services do families welcome and which encourage them in their use? What attributes make these services effective?

Our examination of the current role of mainstream services in preventive work will be undertaken in three stages. Firstly, we shall examine this role in respect of the four themes below. Secondly, using these themes as illustrations, we will ask if there are any common characteristics that bring forth a positive response from families and which suggest services have been effective. Thirdly, we will consider the coordination of services; what we currently know about their effectiveness and what more we need to know.

It is not possible in this report to review all possible work undertaken by mainstream services. We have, therefore, chosen to illustrate this using four themes. These are:

- initiatives to support and enhance the parenting task;
- child health surveillance programmes;
- social service work with children;
- preventing 'anti-social' behaviour in adolescence.

Of necessity we shall look at these themes separately, while recognising that the causes and manifestations of needs of children and families are interlinked.

## *Initiatives to support and enhance the parenting task*

> It is generally agreed that the impact of parenting is felt through-
> out one's lifetime and for succeeding generations. No other form of
> human interaction can boast such power and longevity. (Bavolek,
> 1990)

It is perhaps a truism to say that parents are the key players in
promoting children's optimum development, but the continuing
discussions about whether parenting is 'caught' or can be 'taught'
reflect different views about the extent to which the state should
intervene in the lives of families to support, or improve, family
functioning. In the 1970s, research into a possible 'cycle of deprivation' (Rutter and Madge, 1976) led to proposals for preparation
for parenthood as a possible way of improving parents attitudes
and relationships to their children, thereby, it was hoped breaking this cycle of deprivation (DHSS 1974a and 1974b).

Work at the National Children's Bureau during the 1980s identified a range of initiatives that provided preparation, education
and support for parents and prospective parents (Pugh and
De'Ath 1984). Whilst some of these initiatives were undoubtedly
of value to families caught in the 'cycle of deprivation' and lacking
the 'permitting circumstances' identified by Rutter (1974), a central thrust of the Bureau's study was to recognise the challenges
faced by all parents and the value of parent education being available and accessible to all who wished to take advantage of it – a
primary level service.

A further study published ten years later (Pugh and others,
1994) reported a

> Growing acceptance that parent education and support can offer
> families a range of knowledge, skills and opportunities for devel-
> oping self-confidence and discussing attitudes and approaches
> towards parenting. It must however be based on principles which
> value and respect different approaches to bringing up children, and
> which are relevant and appropriate to fathers as well as mothers.
> (p 213)

This study described a range of educational and supportive
measures, intended to support and enhance the parenting task
with different emphasis at each stage of the life cycle:

● work with young people in schools and youth agencies,
  enabling them to develop trusting and responsible relationships and make choices about their lives;

- the period of transition to parenthood, a particularly vulnerable time for many prospective parents, where there is a greater need for emotional support and health education that is geared to the needs of both parents;
- for parents with children – of all ages – a whole range of initiatives, from information and advice, informal groups and drop-in schemes which help reduce isolation and provide opportunities for sharing experiences and information on bringing up children; through parenting discussion groups; to more highly structured parent education, designed to teach new skills and to change unhelpful patterns of behaviour.

Overviews of parenting programmes (Pugh and others, 1994; Smith and Pugh 1996; Smith, 1996) illustrate the extent to which initiatives in the UK have drawn on the research evidence of the impact on children of parenting styles. This can be summarised as working with parents to:

- develop greater self-awareness;
- improve confidence and self-esteem;
- establish effective boundaries and management methods;
- improve parent-child communication;
- make family life more enjoyable;
- provide useful information on child development.

Programmes aim to support parents to become confident and competent by helping to build up their *knowledge,* to develop their *social and practical skills*, and to develop their *understanding and self-awareness*, whilst recognising the continuing importance of the 'permitting circumstances'.

Smith's study of 38 group parenting programmes (1996) classifies the programmes according to the needs of the parents to whom they are primarily offered and finds three main groups: parents who want to do a 'good enough' job of parenting; parents whose children have behaviour problems, in either the 'normal' range (which any child might be expected to display) or 'severe' range (which may require clinical intervention); and parents with multiple problems and very low self-esteem. Thus programmes fall into all three levels of primary, secondary and tertiary prevention.

These studies found a huge range of organisations and individuals involved in providing parenting programmes.

- education authorities and establishments – nurseries, schools, further education colleges, adult and community education;

- social services – mainly through family centres and other services for 'children in need';
- health agencies – through health visitors, general practitioners, educational and clinical psychologists, child psychiatrists and psychotherapists;
- voluntary organisations – large, small and self-help;
- churches and other faith communities;
- employers.

It should be noted that not all of these services will fall within our definition of mainstream. They were by no means universally available, nor were they all open access: many were specialist services available only on referral from a front-line professional. While such services are needed, if parenting programmes are to play a significant part in preventive work with families these need to more easily available to more families. As Smith and Pugh (1996 p46) conclude:

> If availability and accessibility are to be improved, then it is important that, in addition to the specialist contribution of therapists, psychologists, psychiatrists and social workers, as much provision as possible is available within mainstream services.

Specialist programmes should compliment a much broader picture of community-based support. A recently published survey (FPSC and OPCS 1995) of where parents go for help found that nearly half turned to doctors, health visitors and other health professionals, and one fifth to teachers. Even studies of family centres (Smith, 1995; Statham, 1994; Buchanan 1995) point to the value of community-based open access services which:

> allowed reciprocity to thrive, and the range of coping abilities among families using the centres allows them to support each other (and their community) rather than merely be the recipients of services. (Statham 1994, p27);

A similar view is taken by the Audit Commission (1994) in discussing the role of family centres, it states that 'a mix of open access with a quota of referred families is preferable to a closed system.' (p40).

A small qualitative follow up study to the FPSC/OPCS survey found that parents wanted to be treated in a non-stigmatised way by mainstream services, rather than be the targeted object of intervention. The non-stigmatising advice and gate keeping of health visitors and GPs was seen as critical (Inglis, 1995).

Accessibility and acceptability are key issues in family support, especially if services aim to be mainstream. Many initiatives fail to involve more than a small handful of fathers, despite research which points to the benefits of such programmes (Bronstein and Cowan; 1988); parenting programmes in particular tend to attract white, middle class mothers – with a few notable exceptions such as Exploring Parenthood's Moyenda Project. There is also little support for parents of adolescents. As we note below, there may be other barriers that confront families in accessing services, particularly more vulnerable families. Shinman's study (1981) of access to pre-school services, for example, found that 25 per cent of families would not use a drop-in centre, playgroup or nursery even when it was within easy walking distance, for fear of 'the welfare', levels of depression, low self-esteem, and the difficulties of getting several small children ready to go out. This study has led to wider recognition of the need for community-based outreach/link workers to help vulnerable families with low self-esteem to 'plug into' the system (see Aplin and Pugh 1983; Pugh and Polton 1987). Homestart illustrates this point well: volunteers offer support both to parents and children and, in encouraging parents' strengths and emotional well being, work towards the point when they can widen their network of relationships and use community support and services effectively (van der Eyken 1990, Frost and others, 1996).

As to the effectiveness of parenting education and support, Smith and Pugh (1996) point both to the paucity of rigorous evaluation, but also to the complex range of variables involved in developing a research design. They conclude:

> This study has identified a wide range of approaches and some evaluative studies which show, albeit in a limited way, widespread enjoyment and satisfaction on the part of parents, and reported improvements in relationships and in children's behaviour...parenting programmes make an important contribution to the development of the skills, understanding and the self-confidence of the parents who have participated in them and, through these changes, to the lives of their children. (p 47–48)

They note however, as have comparable American studies (Medway, 1989) that there is no 'best buy'; that different approaches are likely to suit different parents wanting help with different problems.

Most of these studies have focused specifically on parent education, but a review of all the major parent support programmes aimed at 'disadvantaged' families in America concluded that long-term improvement in child development outcomes was only possible in programmes that combined parent support with high quality services for children (Center for Study of Social Policy, 1990). This links into a substantial body of research into parents' role as educators, exemplified in a central message of the longitudinal High/Scope research – that, in addition to the impact of a cognitively orientated curriculum on children's attitudes towards learning and their sense of mastery and self-esteem (Sylva, 1994), 'it is parents' expectation of and interest in their children's education that leads to long-term gains' (Woodhead, 1985).

*Child health surveillance*
Child health surveillance could be said to typify preventive work with families. Since the establishment of the National Health Service, child health surveillance has been available as part of a universal mainstream service, provided free by the State, with open access at local clinics or through home visits by health visitors. These programmes aim to offer advice, monitor progress and identify as early as possible any problems in a child's development.

However in recent years there have been growing challenges to the underlying presumption that preventive services, as currently delivered, actually work or are cost effective (for an overview see Butler, 1989). Here we shall examine some current issues in child health surveillance in *pre-school* children.

Butler notes the diversity and conflict which characterises this activity. There is much evidence that the content, the scale and means of delivery of screening programmes is variable across the country, illustrated by the lack of clarity over the respective roles of health visitors and GPs (MacFarlene and Pillnay, 1984).

Recognising the lack of consensus, a Joint Working Party on child health surveillance with representatives of all the main health professionals was set up in 1986. This body has reviewed research evidence and current practice and made recommendations for future practice. Over the past decade three major reports, have been presented (Hall, 1989, 1991, 1996). These research reviews led to a changed understanding of this aspect of preventive work with families. This has come about for a number of reasons:

• the lack of sound evidence that routine surveillance or health screening was effective;

- a lack of research on the effectiveness of the individual tests;
- major variations in the packages of health surveillance offered by different authorities;
- a lack of confidence in programmes due to evidence of imprecision in the results of tests and low standards in operating the procedures;
- greater appreciation that too little account had been taken of the role of parents in detecting problems in their children;
- too little targeting of families most at risk, especially those within inner cities where mobility is highest.

Despite these reservations the Joint Working Party recommended, and the Department of Health accepted, the continuation of a minimum universally available pre-school health screening programme, supported by other targeted interventions.

Although the actual screening programme recommended in the third report is not greatly different from earlier versions, the tone of these reports changed significantly. This is most noticeable in two respects: the greater focus on primary prevention and a more explicit emphasis on working in partnership with parents.

A greater focus on primary level prevention, especially through active child health promotion, was seen as a necessary complement to a surveillance or screening programme which seeks to detect problems and disorders – a secondary level prevention programme.

In updating their review of research and current practice the latest Working Party report made a number of important recommendations and highlights areas where further research is needed. Some of these points are summarised below, with the identified gaps in research knowledge taken forward into the final section of this report.

The need to view the child holistically and in context is stressed. Studies of children's health have argued that whilst all parents share similar goals for their children, material constraints affect their ability to recognise their goals (Blackburn, 1991; Mayall, 1986). Promoting health in children means taking a broad view of the needs of the child and his or her family, taking account of any social problems, addressing issues of poverty, poor housing and wider public health and environmental issues. It also means recognising the important part in promoting child health that is played by support to families, for instance through day care and drop-in centres. Hence, health promotion is a piece of the overall jigsaw that is preventive work with families.

Child health promotion programmes need to be flexible, but research suggests that some core areas should be pursued by all agencies: breast feeding, post-natal depression, positive parenting, accident prevention, immunisation, nutrition, dental care. While recognising the value of these universal child health promotion programmes the report calls for greater targeting at families most in need. From its examination of the evidence on effectiveness the Working Party argues:

> that doing some things well and in-depth for a few individuals is nearly always more cost-effective than providing a token service to a large number of people. (p30)

This highlights two key issues applicable to any preventive service: identifying those 'few individuals' and ensuring they receive a service; specifying a minimum universal service that is more than simply a 'token'.

These issues were considered by the Audit Commission in respect of the tasks of health visitors and school nurses, with a recommendation for greater task specificity and clearer targeting based on an assessment of need (Audit Commission, 1994). The controversy provoked by these recommendations highlights the enormous complexity in designing and delivering effective preventive services, and as this paper has shown, this is true whatever detriment to children's well-being one is trying to prevent.

The example of health visitors also highlights the issue of selectivity by professionals. Although health visiting is a universal service for parents with young children it is still limited in its resources. This can place health visitors in the role of gatekeeper, free to choose (beyond the 12-day statutory visit) who they work with and who they do not. This may have the unintended consequence of effectively excluding or undermining some families, for instance, those who display aggressive behaviour. This highlights the complexity of ensuring that all families, including those who do not manifest 'acceptable' behaviours, have access to professionals and to services at the earliest stage of need. Failure to do this means the level of need escalates and intervention is determined by a legally framed requirement, such as a child protection investigation or police/court intervention.

It is clear that child health promotion, whether at primary or secondary level of prevention, can only be effective if professionals work in partnership with parents. In essence this acknowledges the shift from *telling* parents and families what to do – to one of *asking, consulting with, listening to, advising* parents (Sutton and others, 1995). This is well demonstrated by the evaluation of a Child Development Programme (Barker and others, 1994). Specially trained health visitors used monthly home visits to work with new mothers to provide them with workable strategies for child rearing and promoting the health of their children. In a similar programme, *Community Mothers*, subject to a random control trial, more mature experienced mothers were used as supporters. This study showed positive results, for instance in terms of the take-up of immunisations, diet management and constructive child/parent activity and relationships (Johnson and others, 1995).

In reviewing research on work with parents, the Working Party noted the emphasis on mothers and identified the role of fathers and the relationship of professionals with fathers as an area needing greater attention; again an issue which resonates in all the topic areas we have examined (Burgess and Ruxton, 1996).

From reviews of evaluations of health promotion programmes from across cultures and populations, it is possible to identify a set of common features in services which parents rate highly (Larner and others, 1992). See Figure 7 below.

---

**Figure 7    Characteristics of successful health promotion programmes as identified by parents**

- Services are broad spectrum and comprehensive, crossing traditional professional boundaries, and are coherent and easy to use;
- Structures and individual staff are flexible in their ability to respond to unexpected demands;
- Staff have time and skill to establish a relationship of respect and trust with families;
- The child is seen as a member of the family, the family as part of a community;
- Enthusiastic committed leadership, clearly specified measurable aims and focus on families with high levels of need;
- Sustained high quality input and sufficient *continuity* of input to develop a relationship with the individual client.

---

So what do these research findings mean for the design and delivery of services? First the need for coordination, for multi-agency, multi-disciplinary services – the building of *Healthy*

*Alliances* (DH, 1993). For instance, how is child health promotion linked to parent education, family support or community development? What are the component tasks? What skills are needed to deliver child health promotion? Which professional or professional mixes or lay people are best placed to do this? From what agency or community base? These are issues we will return to when we have examined two further examples of preventive work with families.

## Social service work with children

Since the 1948 Child Care Act, preventive work with children has had a fluctuating place within social work practice. Even in the more idealistic 1960s and 1970s few local authorities played a significant role in primary prevention – in 'the maintenance of a social infrastructure that supports parents in the tasks of bringing up their children' (Williamson, 1995).

With the continuing spotlight on child abuse inquiries in the 1970s and 1980s many social work practitioners and managers felt compelled to emphasise protection of children, often through statutory social work intervention. At the same time many parents seeking help were faced with stringent gatekeeping of the care system and with few alternatives on offer (Packman and others, 1986; Bunyan and Sinclair, 1987). If we add to this severe financial constraints, we find 'preventive' work with families was mostly at the tertiary or quaternary level – with the principal goal of prevention of admission to the care system or 'permanency' (Thorpe, 1988).

The Barclay Report (*Task and Roles of Social Workers*, 1982) confirmed and developed the Seebohm Report's emphasis on early, multiskilled interventions as part of the social work repertoire. However, the fact that there was no mandatory authority attached to the findings of the Barclay Committee meant that the development of 'community social work' was ad hoc and reliant on the vision of managers and the preferences of practitioners. Many teams developed ways of working which achieved reductions in the need for tertiary and quaternary interventions (Smale and others, 1989, 1990). However, how these changes were achieved was often not sufficiently understood, nor were they subject to formal evaluation of their apparent success.

Research continued to show that the needs of many children coming into the care system related as much to material deprivation and lack of family support as wilful neglect or maltreatment and that compulsorily separating children from their families was in general harmful and only necessary in a minority of cases (Holman, 1980; DHSS, 1985; Packman, 1986; Parker and others, 1991; DH, 1995).

The Children Act 1989 set out to reconcile the competing demands of 'safeguarding' children and 'promoting' their welfare, to bridge the division between 'protection' and 'prevention'. It aimed to do this by giving to local authorities the clear duty to safeguard and promote the welfare of children in need, affirming the responsibilities of parents and enhancing the rights of children when their welfare became the concern of courts and the public authorities. In family court proceedings a child's welfare was deemed paramount. The Act established a principle of working in partnership with parents and by recognising the duty of the State to support families in their tasks of bringing up children. However in the Act, 'support' was not intended as a universal service for all children and families but one that was reserved for those children deemed to be 'children in need'. Nonetheless the duty imposed on local authorities by Section 17 of the Children Act 'to safeguard and promote the welfare of children within their area who are in need by providing a range and level of services appropriate to those children's needs,' provided the opportunity for a major shift in the role of social services departments (SSDs) in preventive work with families. As Packman and Jordan expressed it 'the Act takes a quantum leap from the old restrictive notions of 'prevention' to a more positive outreaching duty of 'support for children and families' (Packman and Jordan, 1991).

The Children Act strongly encouraged local authorities to extend the range of family support services, including the provision of family centres, drop-in centres and after school care. So how has this new 'support to families' worked in practice? The findings of the study on the implementation of Section 17 suggests that there is much more to be done if this part of the Act is to be meaningful (Aldgate and Tunstill, 1995). While the researchers identified changes in some local authorities in terms of an expanding criteria for access to services, the picture was very varied. By and large SSDs reported that due to resource constraints support to families was still confined to children deemed to be 'at risk', with few new services to those 'in need'. Similar limitations seem to apply to the use of accommodation under Section 20 of the Children Act, which is most likely to be used when family breakdown is a real possibility or has effectively occurred (Bradley and others, 1994) rather than when stress can be alleviated and a family sustained.

The role of SSD family support services in relation to preventive work with families needs further consideration. What role can social services departments play in primary prevention? This was the specific focus of a study by Gibbons (1990). This confirmed that family centres of the 'neighbourhood type' (Holman, 1988) do seem to be effective in promoting family well-being. It is more difficult to demonstrate their impact on the prevention of specific problems. The very open access nature of these centres means that while they may be located in identified neighbourhoods, they may not be reaching families with severe problems. Can these primary prevention services have sufficient impact where families are experiencing problems? Do families most in need make use of such services? If not, and there is some evidence to suggest this is the case, how can they be encouraged to use them? Can primary, mainstream services promote the introduction of families with more specific needs to secondary preventive services? Certainly this would be a claim of the Pen Green Centre, a multi-level service in Birmingham which has been clearly documented, although not yet subject to external evaluation (Whalley, 1994 and 1996).

Consideration of the contribution of social services to preventive work with families also leads us to look at the relationship between Part III of the Children Act – support for children and families – to that of Part V – protection of children. In terms of the allocation of social workers most authorities operate a clear hierarchy – with child protection top priority, children looked after next and only if resources permit, other children in need (Barn, Sinclair and Ferdinand, 1997). Of course not all support to families requires a social work input, but often this acts as the 'gate' to other resources. This hierarchy is reinforced by social services jargon which still refers to 'non-statutory' work when this is not child protection or children looked after (Aldgate and Tunstill, 1995); this is despite the clear statutory duty in Section 17 of the Children Act to promote the welfare of children in need.

The recent review of research on the operation of the child protection system suggests that child protection investigations and the offer of family support are viewed as alternatives although this was not the intention of the Children Act (DH, 1995). For instance, the study by Gibbons and others (1995), found that six out of seven children who enter the child protection system were filtered out during the investigation process and that 75 per cent of those families who were brought into the child protection investigative process (under Section 47 of the Children Act) actually received no preventive or supportive help under Section 17 of the Act.

The challenge of 'refocusing practice' in social work is to ensure that those who may be screened out as not necessarily needing third or fourth level preventive services, are at least assured of access to second or primary level services – what may be termed family support services. The tendency for child protection services to be viewed as both primary intervention and at the 'heavy end' of working with families has a major impact on the ability of more mainstream social services such as field teams to contribute to preventive work with families.

There is now much evidence to suggest that families who recognise their need for help are afraid to seek it from social services because they fear, rightly in many cases, the instigation of a child protection investigation.

Similarly many young people who run away from abusive situations at home, do so in preference to contacting social services which they perceive as intrusive in a negative way (Barker, 1996). This young runaway clearly expresses the views of many in need of help.

> 'You never, ever talk to social worker. That's just how it is... . They're like the police but they don't wear uniforms. You just keep out of their way.'

A key aspect of refocusing practice must relate to the image that social services presents to families and that consequently support may be inhibited by its co-existence within social service departments with traditionally delivered child protection services. There is a great deal of work to be done to ensure that prevention and support is seen as the context within which a protective intervention may occur rather than as an alternative (Hearn, 1995; Parton, 1985).

## Preventing anti-social behaviour in adolescents

The image of teenagers, especially as portrayed by the media, is often an unsympathetic one. Yet for teenagers and their families the adolescent years can be difficult. Adolescence is a period characterised by uncertainty, ambiguity of status, confusion over boundaries and, for many young people, as a time of increased vulnerability. Problems that may have been developing for some time can become manifest in adolescence in terms of family relationship difficulties, school-related problems, anti-social behaviour or psycho-social disorder. While teenagers are more likely to be seen as a source of problems, they are as likely to be victims. For instance, the peak age at which young people start to commit offences is 15 years, (Home Office, 1995) but adolescents are also most likely to be victims of crime with young people aged 12-15 more likely than older teenagers or adults to be the victims of offending behaviour (Aye Maung, 1995). In looking at preventive work with families we shall concentrate on reducing anti-social behaviour in adolescence.

There is certainly a growing body of literature reporting on the extent, the nature and some of the risk factors associated with adolescents' behaviour – for example, the major review of research by Rutter and Smith (1995) into psycho-social disorders in anti-social behaviour in young people over the past 50 years; research on school exclusions and bullying in school (see Parsons, 1996; Smith and Sharp, 1994); and the continuing body of research on youth crime (see, Graham and Bowling, 1995; Farrington, 1994). All of this points to the inter-relationship between families and school and behaviour in adolescence. There is also evidence to suggest a link between general anti-social behaviour and offending, although the exact nature of that relationship is far from clear (Farrington, 1996). Here we will limit our discussion to criminal behaviour.

Interventions aimed at the prevention of offending are likely to be needed at all levels. Youth crime is a widespread phenomenon with almost half of all 14- to 25-years-olds having committed at least one offence. This suggests that interventions which are universally targeted are likely to be effective, where the focus of these interventions is on those factors thought to relate to the onset of offending behaviour. The importance of developing effective primary prevention strategies with young people is reinforced by research which links the onset of offending at an early age to a long standing criminal career. Preventive work aimed at persuading those who have committed crime to desist will require a more focused strategy – for instance aimed at neighbourhoods with high crime rates and again linked to identified risk and protective factors. However these primary and secondary preventive measures are unlikely to be effective, on their own, for the small proportion of very persistent offenders. This will require third level preventive strategies, and the deployment of services outside the mainstream.

There is a substantial body of knowledge which can help to identify those factors associated with both the onset of criminal behaviour and continuing criminality. However there is much less evidence of the effectiveness of particular interventions. In a major overview of research on preventing youth crime, Farrington (1996) reports on the dearth of outcome studies in the UK and relies on American evaluation research for suggested prevention strategies: intensive home visiting; parent skills education; pre-school intellectual enrichment; peer influence resistance strategies: anti-bullying programmes in schools; situational crime prevention. These strategies relate closely to Home Office research (Graham and Bowling, 1995) which identifies four interlinked factors associated with the onset of offending in young people, confirming those of other studies. The four factors are:

- low parental supervision;
- truancy and exclusion from school;
- having friends and/or siblings who are in trouble with the police;
- poor family attachment.

This study also suggests that once offending starts the role of family and school is less important than peer influence, again suggesting the need for different interventions at the primary and secondary level.

What contribution do mainstream services make to preventing criminality by reducing the impact of these predictive factors? What contribution could they make? We will look at each of these four 'risk' factors, but will consider low parental supervision and poor family attachment together.

**Low parental supervision and poor family attachment:** Both these aspects are linked to parenting styles. Research has demonstrated the impact of different parenting styles on the outcomes for young people (see p4). What we are less sure about is why parents adopt particular styles or how these can be influenced or changed. Here the role of mainstream services is likely to be in supporting and educating parents, as discussed earlier.

In considering the interplay between child/parent relationships and offending two further questions need to be asked. First, what is the role of fathers? Offending behaviour in young men is particularly associated with a poor relationship between boys and their fathers **or by modelling the criminal behaviour of a father.** To what extent does this feature in current parent education programmes? How do young fathers learn their parenting skills? How can we use existing knowledge about fatherhood to address this issue? (see Burgess and Ruxton, 1996). Second, while the seeds of child/parent relationships are sown early in a child's life, problems often manifest themselves at a later stage. What mainstream services are available for teenagers and their parents offering ongoing support and to help them address relationship difficulties? How accessible, how acceptable, how effective are these? The limited evidence to respond to these questions highlights the need for both research and development initiatives.

**School exclusions:** these have risen rapidly, reaching over 11,000 per year in 1995/96. At less than half of one per cent of all secondary school pupils this represents the crisis end of non-school attendance. Truancy, disaffection and under-achievement are the more common precursors which, if not dealt with, are likely to lead to an exclusion. It is here that mainstream services have to make a contribution if they are to prevent the need for a crisis-oriented response from a specialist service. For instance, Hagel and Newburn (1994) in their study on *Persistent Offenders* indicated that unidentified problems with reading seem to arise more frequently in this population. OFSTED spells out what schools can do to reduce exclusions – implementing effective behaviour policies, applying suitable rewards and sanctions and tailoring their curriculum to meet individual needs and the key role to be played by LEAs especially in monitoring, training and the provision of support services (OFSTED, 1996).

School-related problems may arise from factors external to the school, such as family dysfunction, deprivation or mental health problems, or internal such as poor school discipline, bullying or inappropriate curriculum (Hayden, 1994; Blyth and Miller, 1994; Elton, 1989; Sammons and others, 1995). In reviewing the home and family circumstances of excluded pupils OFSTED reported 'a grim catalogue of misery' – poverty, loss of parents through death or family breakdown, absentee fathers, sick parents, physical, sexual or racial abuse (OFSTED, 1996). Given these disparate factors the focus of preventive work must be equally diverse, involving a range of services, which need to be coordinated and take account of the views of pupils (Graham, 1988; Pitts and Smith, 1995; Malek, 1996; Kinder and others, 1996; Makins, 1997).

A major initiative to help schools is the GEST programme on truancy and disaffected pupils. While this does provide additional resources that appear useful, the scheme seems to be under-funded, fragmented and with insufficient dissemination of 'good practice' (DfEE, 1995, Learmouth, 1995). Other primary preven-tion resources, such as home-school work are equally piece-meal (Bastiani and Wolfendale, 1996; Malek, 1996).

There is growing involvement of the voluntary and private sector in initiatives to maintain young people in schools (for instance, Cities in Schools; East London Schools Fund, Schools Outreach) and early intervention programmes to support chil-dren in school such as the National Pyramid Trust, Spring Board, the place to be (see Malek, forthcoming, 1997). These programmes are often carrying out tasks once undertaken within mainstream school activity or by services such as the Education Welfare Ser-vice, indicating the increasing inability of statutory agencies to engage in preventive work. There is some evidence that in respect of truants that the police are adopting an approach that is less punitive and more collaborative (Lewis, 1996).

We indicated that many problems which manifest in school are caused elsewhere, in the home, through relationship or mental health problems. However it seems that other agencies are not likely to be involved until a crisis is reached. More needs to be done to ensure that others, in particular social services, identify these young people as 'children in need' under the Children Act and play an effective role at an earlier stage.

**Delinquent friends:** the influence of delinquent friends on offending suggests the need for preventive activity that is tar-geted at groups or neighbourhoods and which offers attractive alternatives for young people. This resonates with the views of young offenders in Wiltshire who identified the lack of activity and boredom, as the main barriers to keeping them out of trouble (Buchanan, 1995) and supports the strong subjective evidence found in a study of the Youth Service which revealed 'a consensus that effective and focused youth work had a valuable contribution to play in diverting young people from crime' (Coopers and Lybrand, 1994). The Audit Commission noted great variation in the resources devoted to youth work by local authorities, and in the services provided. Most youth workers viewed their role as providing a universal service, although some authorities had specifically targeted their efforts at vulnerable young people, an approached recommended by the Audit Commission (1996). However there is little objective evidence of the role of youth work or of sport or physically demanding activity in effective crime prevention (Robbins, 1980). More research is needed on the contribution of these activities; what seems to make them attractive and able to retain the interest of which groups of young people?

**Coordinating efforts to prevent delinquency:** in reviewing the prevention of juvenile offending we have looked at four 'risk' factors independently. However it is increasingly clear that isolated interventions are less likely to be useful. What is required is a programme of interventions that includes a range of initiatives, operating at different prevention levels and focusing on different aspects of a child's life. But within any one area these initiatives are properly coordinated to allow sufficient breadth and momentum to effect changes. As Farrington (1996) says 'there is a growing consensus among researchers and policy makers on the value of applying a general programmatic method to crime prevention'. It would seem that the time is right for the introduction of such an experimental programme together with a carefully designed evaluation, a theme we discuss more fully in the next section.

The Audit Commisssion has reviewed the resources expended by public agencies in dealing with young offenders and concluded that there is an inappropriate and inefficient allocation of resources to later rather than early intervention. They recommend more preventive work within mainstream services.

> Resources need to be shifted from processing young offenders to dealing with their behaviour, while efforts to prevent offending and other anti-social behaviour need to be piloted, evaluated, coordinated and targeted on the deprived areas with high crime rates. (Audit Commission, 1996)

### Mainstream services and preventive work

From this brief overview of preventive work what conclusions can we draw about the role of mainstream services? First, that mainstream services, whether in the statutory or independent sectors, are fundamental to preventive work with families. Second, in all four areas reviewed there are currently significant limitations on the role that mainstream services are playing. There are many reasons why this is so:

- parenting education and support is patchy and certainly not universally available; those least well served are fathers, people from minority ethnic groups and parents of older children and young people;
- while child health assessment needs to be universal and mainstream, the health visiting service is insufficiently targeted, in either the people it serves or its input, to ensure that those in greatest need, who may resist help, get an adequate and appropriate service;
- the capacity of social services to increase their role in preventive work is inhibited by the skills and experience of their staff and resource allocation priorities which still favour child protection services, despite debates on 'refocusing practice'; social services are further inhibited in preventive work by their image, which makes them unacceptable to many families as a source of help;
- much is now known about the 'risk' factors related to the onset of anti-social behaviour in adolescence. Efforts to prevent this are limited by the lack of parenting support noted above; the decreasing capacity for mainstream statutory services to provide early intervention through supportive services to prevent problems in schools escalating; declining youth services; poor coordination between service providers; insufficient momentum in interventions to generate change; and again by resources expended on the results of anti-social behaviour rather than its prevention.

This overview also suggests that whatever the problem we are trying to prevent that there are common themes that should inform our approach to preventive work. So what are the overarching messages that we need to take forward to future agendas?

- the need to work *with* families, to build self-esteem and to enable them to identify their needs and how these can be addressed;
- the need to achieve the right balance between universal and targeted services to ensure that those most in need can benefit from primary prevention;
- the development of interventions that are coordinated and which successfully interlink services delivered by all sectors and agencies and at all preventive levels;
- the essential requirement that new services or ways of working are evaluated, indicating which services are effective for which particular families or young people.

# 4. Attributes of effective preventive services

We have illustrated the contribution of mainstream services to preventive work by examining four apparently distinct areas of social intervention. What becomes clear is the interconnection between these areas: of the overlap in risk and protective factors; in the common messages about attributes of services which users value and find effective; and in the importance of coordinating services. These are the themes of this section.

Evaluation studies repeatedly demonstrate that to be effective, preventive social interventions need to be clear about the aims of the intervention and what they are trying to achieve. Yet when we review these interventions with different aims, the close inter-relationship of issues is very apparent – particularly the pivotal importance of the child/parent or carer relationship. Furthermore these reviews show the limited impact that can be expected from isolated preventive activity and the added value from interlinking interventions. Effective change requires more than a one-off injection or un-dimensional input (see for instance review of child accident preventions, Nuffield Health Unit for Review, 1996).

The Audit Commission concluded that breaking into the cycle of anti-social behaviour in young people required a comprehensive range of interventions, as illustrated in Figure 8. Similarly Utting and colleagues proposed, also in respect of crime prevention, what they termed as a 'family-based delinquency prevention programme' (see Figure 9). This model offers a multi-level approach addressing a wide range of potential areas of difficulty, from many angles – including work on parenting skills, on management in schools, in enhancing access to health care and promotion. The model also addresses the changing needs of families at different ages and stages of childhood. Perhaps the Utting programme includes too little that is aimed at the current needs of adolescents, and these elements of the Audit Commission model could usefully be added to this.

**Figure 8    Breaking into the cycle of anti-social behaviour**

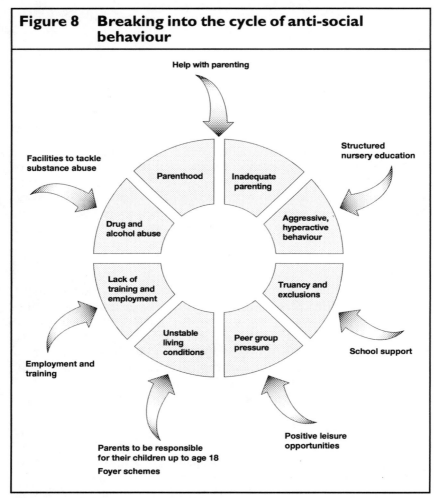

**Source:** *Misspent Youth* Audit Commission 1996

In many ways the individual interventions suggested here are not new, and examples can be found here and there throughout Britain. A recent Home Office study identifies a range of such initiatives currently operating in Britain. Although the authors acknowledge that few have been subject to rigorous evaluation they believe that all demonstrate promise in working to reduce criminality (Utting, 1997). What would be new would be the availability of the total package within one specific area – and a programme to monitor and evaluate it.

Even with this multi-level approach, a considerable challenge – and one which runs throughout this report – is how to meet the needs of all children, whilst at the same time focusing sufficiently to meet the particular needs of the most vulnerable children.

If that challenge is to be met, then in terms of our previous analogy, the construction of the fence at the top of the cliff must be appropriate. It must be of a style that attracts all those who can benefit; it must be strong enough so those in greatest need don't fall through; and it must act as a guiding rail to channel those who require a more specialist service in the right direction.

## Figure 9   A family-based delinquency prevention programme

**Universal**
- Family planning and preparation for family life education in schools;
- Ante- and post-natal care, guiding new parents into networks of support and advice;
- A national, mass-media campaign on parent education;
- Access to parental skills training courses (publicly subsidised where necessary);
- Good quality, affordable child care available for parents who choose to work;
- Pre-school education of a high-quality, in partnership with parents;
- 'Effectiveness' programmes in primary and secondary school, ensuring minimum reading/mathematical skills and maintaining liaison with parents;
- Strategies to prevent bullying in schools.

**Neighbourhood**
- Open access family centres offering relevant services such as parent and toddler clubs; playgroups; toy libraries; parent training; money advice; after-school clubs; special group work (such as for victims of domestic violence, mothers who have been in care); family therapy;
- Remedial design work and improved management of high crime estates;
- Community policing, including preventive work with families;
- Clubs and holiday activities for children and young people;
- Participation of parents in the management of family centres, schools and other community projects.

**Home**
- Extension of health visits to the parents of young children as well as infants;
- Befriending, babysitting and other outreach services – perhaps organised from neighbourhood family centres;
- Family support volunteers, improving the ability of parents under stress to cope (such as Home-Start);
- Family preservation services, providing intensive support for families in the shadow of care proceedings (such as Newpin, Radford Shared Care Project and Michigan 'Families First').

**Source:** *Crime and the Family* (Utting and others, 1993)

This overview of preventive services provides some consistent messages which suggests how the fence should be constructed – about the attributes of services that seem to be successful. In Figure 10, we identify these attributes in terms of **seven A's** and discuss them below.

| Figure 10      Attributes of effective services |
| --- |
| • Available<br>• Acceptable<br>• Affordable<br>• Accessible<br>• Accountable<br>• Appropriate<br>• Across-agency |

While these attributes are drawn from studies cited in this report, there is little evidence to suggest that most services are characterised by these attributes. The challenge, then, is to develop policy and change practice to reflect what we know to be effective in working in preventive ways with more vulnerable families.

**Available:** services are only going to be of use if they are available; yet, with the exception of schools, primary health care and ante-natal clinics, many of the universal services listed in Figure 10 above are not universally available. The reasons for this derive in part from practice of service development, in part from resource allocation.

*Practice development:* new approaches too often rely on the inspiration of individuals yet at no, or very limited, additional cost, this could be replicated widely. For instance, personal and social education, including preparation for family life, could become part of the school curriculum; just as strategies to prevent bullying could be developed in all schools.

*Service development:* equally, some community-based early childhood centres are able to offer both open access nursery care and education, and informal support for parents, as well as specialised therapeutic support for those whose needs are greatest (Whalley, 1993; Makins, 1997).

How can initiatives such as these be more widely disseminated and become incorporated as mainstream? Can we identify the elements in such initiatives that are transferable and generalisable to other situations?

*Resources:* as public expenditure comes under the microscope, questions are asked about how much welfare can still be afforded, which services consumers should be required to pay for, what should be cut and what areas, if any, could be expanded. In reviewing the benefits and costs of increasing our investment in children, Holtermann (1995a) concluded that more could be done to enhance the well being of children, but that it would need a willingness to increase public expenditure and taxation. The issue, then, is one of political will.

Additionally, the size of the task would require a level of investment of time, ideas, and action that would mean complex realignment within and between agencies. The problems of scale in achieving change are, for example, reflected in the failure to comprehensively implement the Elton Committee recommendations on school discipline, or to take forward the pledge on nursery education made by Mrs Thatcher back in 1972 (DES, 1972; DES, 1989).

How can we ensure that support services for children receive adequate priority in resource allocation? How can the level of mainstream preventive services be maintained and where necessary increased?

**Acceptable:** if families are to use services, they must be acceptable to them. Research cited above suggests that services must:

- be non-stigmatising, not identifying families as 'failures';
- work with parents and/or young people 'where they are at' rather than where service providers feel they ought to be and building on their strengths;
- listen to the views of parents, children and young people;
- enable parents, children and young people to participate or engage in the scheme or service in the way that suits them;
- empower and enable parents, acknowledging and building on their skills, abilities and experience rather than increasing feelings of anxiety and guilt;
- encourage reciprocity – enabling families to support each other, to give as well as take;
- be acceptable to fathers as well as mothers, boys as well as girls, young men as well as young women;
- reflect and respect individual families' ethnicity, religion, language and culture, understanding different childrearing practices, and employing staff from the communities they serve.

What are the current barriers to adopting these approaches? What are the implications of this approach for service delivery and the training of staff who work with families? How can the views of children and families be heard in planning and developing services?

**Affordable:** to be effective services must be affordable. If services that are of value in promoting the welfare of children and families – such as day care and nursery education – are beyond the reach of most family budgets, then they are also unavailable to most. If such services were universal Holtermann estimates that a third of parents could afford to pay, a third would need a full subsidy and a third a part subsidy – which could be repaid to the Exchequer as parents or carers return to work (Holtermann, 1995b).

If preventive services are not free, what subsidies should be available? How best can subsidies be accessed, to encourage their use without creating stigma? How can poorer families gain access to preventive services which exact a charge such as counselling or family therapy or health promoting activities?

**Accessible:** accessibility is most obviously linked to physical distances, but it relates to the other barriers that confront families in accessing services, particularly more vulnerable families. Such barriers include:

- distance from the family's home and lack of transport;
- personal attributes and circumstances, for example poor self-image, fear of the 'welfare', isolation and depression;
- cultural/ethnic and social/class barriers presented by a service that does not respect/reflect the family's culture or lifestyle;
- lack of translation/interpretation services;
- inconvenient times at which the service is available;
- lack of a creche for parents of young children;
- inaccessible professional jargon;
- reliance on too much written material;
- denial that there is a problem, or different views about what the problem is;
- financial barriers (as discussed above).

How well do service planners and practitioners understand the needs of those who may benefit from a service? Do we ask why some people do not use a service? Is outreach work sufficiently valued? What are the implications of these barriers for the training of staff?

**Accountable:** our definition of mainstream included the requirement that services be subject to specific inspection and regulation – a key aspect of accountability. The Children Act, a series of Education Acts and the Citizen's Charter have all emphasised the importance of services being accountable to parents, though there has been rather less attention paid to the rights of children as consumers. Not all parents or young people will want to be on the management committee of a service, but all will want to be taken seriously, to have their views listened to, and to be given regular feedback and open access to information. Whilst there have been many improvements – for example in the reporting procedures of schools to parents, and in the setting up of contracts between purchasers and providers of services – much still remains to be done.

**Appropriate:** services must be appropriate to families, not only in terms of the level of prevention and the nature of problem, but most importantly in relation to the needs of parents and their children. Work in four schools in Birmingham, for example, started from an assumption that parents wanted 'wrap-around' day care; in fact when asked they said they first needed access to training and support with parenting (Birmingham SSD 1995). Similarly, Ferri and Saunders (1991) and Cannan (1992) both found disparity between social workers who thought parents should have parenting skills training, and parents who wanted child care, time off from their children, opportunities for their children to play with others, and someone to talk to. So for services to be appropriate, providers will need to:

- ask parents, children and young people what they want;
- remember that these needs will vary over time, so continue to ask on a regular basis;
- recognise that needs will also be different at different stages of the life cycle and in different parenting situations: that parents of adolescents or young people themselves will have very different needs from the parents of a first baby; that step-parents or adoptive parents or grandparents will have specific needs as will those families from the diverse range of ethnic and religious communities;
- be flexible in what is offered, where it is offered, how it is offered (language used) and when it is offered (the hours available);
- consider that what parents want may not be the same as what professionals think is good for them and that each parent may have a different perspective.

**Across-agency:** children and their parents seldom see their needs as separate components of education, health, welfare, housing, play –

more often the support or advice that they require draws on the resources of many agencies. Multi-agency responses to families can:

- meet the needs of children and young people as a whole, perhaps through a 'one-stop shop' approach;
- promote a joint approach to assessment of need;
- jointly plan, fund and deliver services;
- prevent overlap and gaps between services;
- make the best possible use of resources;
- ensure that services provide for a whole range of families, not just the most needy – they address primary, secondary and tertiary prevention;
- provide better information to families about the availability of services;
- enable professionals working with families to share skills and expertise, for instance to improve the service to people from a minority ethnic community, where one agency has the necessary experience to enhance the skills of another which does not.

In this seventh A, as in the other six, we must ask why it is proving so difficult to use the evidence that we have to improve the effectiveness of services for families and children? How do we overcome the barriers to coordination of services – between different agencies, different sectors and different levels of prevention?

At a practice level there are countless examples of collaboration – truancy initiatives which bring community police officers together with schools, health visitors liaising with housing officers, motor projects for teenagers and so on. Yet too often collaboration depends on one or two individuals; links may be isolated and difficult to sustain.

Similarly at a local level there are many instances of collaboration between agencies – health centres or GP practice which employ social workers, schools that employ health professionals, social services departments that employ teachers and so on – but individual initiatives are seldom able to overcome the lack of interagency strategic planning (Lloyd, 1994).

It is not difficult to identify potential barriers to joint working across education, health and social services and youth service:

- different legislative frameworks;
- the volume of legislative change which has affected all agencies, leading to a preoccupation with their own organisational issues;
- different professional values and priorities;

- different language/vocabulary;
- different management styles and organisational culture;
- different geographical and statutory boundaries;
- different training and conditions of service;
- lack of shared, achievable goals;
- pressures of time;
- lack of confidence and trust;
- ignorance about other services.

A very similar list is possible in respect of cross sectorial work between statutory, voluntary and private sector agencies. So the challenge of creating an across-agency approach to preventive work with families is great. One such initiative is currently underway in Manchester where education and social services are developing a comprehensive strategy for all children with a key role for schools in providing the base for an inter-agency family support service (Rea Price and Pugh, 1995).

Rarely is there any systematic evaluation of such collaborative initiatives, whatever the level. It is therefore difficult either to judge their effectiveness and for whom, to assess whether or which elements of an approach are transferable, to learn how the barriers to change can be overcome and to work to do so in a systematic way.

# 5. Evaluating social interventions

This overview has been about more than merely describing the contribution of mainstream services to preventive work; it has included implicit reference to the effectiveness of such interventions. Demonstrating 'what works' is complex and it is not intended to dwell on matters of research design here. These issues are already the subject of much debate (see MacDonald and Roberts, 1995; Oakley and Roberts, 1996; Cullen and Hill, 1997). However before moving to propose a research and development agenda for preventive work with families it is worth noting some methodological issues which have informed our thinking. That is the purpose of this section.

Evaluating social interventions can be undertaken for a number of reasons and can be addressed in a variety of ways. For instance 'process' evaluations will ask different questions than 'outcome' evaluations or those exploring cost-effectiveness. What is important is understanding the nature of those questions, valid and reliable ways of answering them, and interpreting and using those answers appropriately.

We have already remarked upon the noted lack of methodologically robust studies which demonstrate clearly the impact or outcomes from preventive work – or how these outcomes may differ depending on individual characteristics. We have been able to refer more often to studies which describe service interventions – the nature of the service, who they are aimed at and who receives them. We have mentioned studies which tell us about the relationship between inputs and outputs and the processes in between. Increasingly these include the views of the users and their assessment of both the quality and the effectiveness of the service. Each of these study types has a part, albeit a different part, to play in understanding the contribution of mainstream services to preventive work.

The paucity of robust studies reflects both a lack of committment and the complexity of evaluating the effectiveness of social interventions; this is especially so with primary preventions where the ability to determine recipients and control the exact nature of the intervention is more limited.

At one end of the spectrum of research designs are those which are capable of demonstrating with confidence an attributable causal relationship between a clearly defined and controlled intervention and subsequent changes or outcomes usually through random control trials. Clear methodological quality criteria have been established in the health field for assessing such effectiveness studies (Cochrane Centre, 1994). These are:

- a clear definition of aims;
- a detailed description of the process of intervention to facilitate effective replication;
- inclusion of a randomly allocated control group;
- data on numbers of participants in the study and control groups;
- provision of pre-intervention data for both groups;
- provision of post-intervention data for both groups;
- attrition rates for both groups;
- findings on each outcome measure as set out in the aims of the study.

These so called 'gold standard' criteria are rarely met nor are they always relevant or applicable. For instance, in reviewing research on sexual health education for young people, Oakley and colleagues assessed only four out of 65 studies as reaching this standard (Oakley and others, 1995). Similar findings are true for social work (MacDonald, Sheldon and Gillespie, 1992). Few of the studies are British, most are American. Some of the difficulties in random control trials relate to ethical and practical problems in random allocation; to problems in specifying and controlling the intervention and the rate of attrition; the scale, length and therefore cost of such experiments.

Nonetheless studies which are seen to be methodologically robust can be undertaken successfully and can be very powerful, as demonstrated by the research on the High/Scope Curriculum in the Perry Pre-schools Programme (Hohmamm, Banet and Weikart, 1976). This study is influential because the longitudinal design is capable of relating early years interventions to behaviour in adolescence and young adults (see Berrueta-Clement, and others, 1984; Schweinhert, Barnes and Weikart, 1993). However the value of longitudinal studies can be reduced by the speed of social change. This may mean that even if significant relationships can be shown between early events and later outcomes, these results may be irrelevant if the earlier conditions are no longer existent or replicable. This may be a factor in assessing the current relevance of the findings from longitudinal studies which explore family structures (Burghes, 1994). The applicability of such studies also needs to be judged in respect of the relevance of the cultural context (Woodhead, 1985).

Concerns are also expressed about the narrowness of the variables that may be measured in very complex social interventions. In their overview of 'what works in the early years' Macdonald and Roberts include other less methodologically rigorous research methods (Macdonald and Roberts, 1995). These research designs, while not capable of 'proving' a direct cause and effect can nonetheless be valid in suggesting likely relationships. As stated earlier, what is important is that the research methods used are compatible with the research questions asked and the reporting of the resultant findings.

This is particularly important in respect of the transferability or generalisation of findings. For example Harman and Brim (1980) in their review of evaluations of parent education programmes note the dangers of over generalisation, of applying the results from evaluations of specific programmes too broadly or in a different context.

One of the difficulties in assessing the effectiveness of interventions is defining outcomes. In unravelling the concept of outcomes in child care, Parker and colleagues (1991) propose three questions which need to be asked. Firstly, for whom is something considered to be an outcome? They suggest in child care there are potentially five outcome perspectives:

- outcomes for the child;
- family outcomes;
- professional outcomes;
- service outcomes;
- public outcomes.

The second question asks, in how much detail should outcomes be specified? The third matter to be determined is the timescale over which the outcome will be measured. Are we measuring immediate outcomes, outcomes after one or two years or long term outcomes?

For instance policy makers may feel that public funded interventions can only be justified when they can demonstrate long term changes; for users of services and their families the fact that they are receiving a good service now, one that meets their immediate needs, may be sufficient justification.

Consideration of outcomes points to the importance of understanding the impact of an intervention from the perspective of all of those involved; what may be termed the different stakeholders' perspectives (Guba and Lincoln, 1989).

Particularly important is research based on users' views. While some would argue that such studies won't provide the same level of 'objective' measurement of change or of causal relationships as experimental approaches they do provide very valid documentation of the impact of an intervention as judged by those children and families involved. The working party on child health surveillance stressed the importance of evidence-based practice, and recognised the validity of users' views.

> There are some aspects of preventive child health that will always be difficult to measure.... At the same time, the concerns and preoccupations of parents must be considered; services perceived as valuable by the 'consumer' should not be too readily dismissed even if evidence of effectiveness is scanty. (Hall, 1996)

Equally important is enabling the child to communicate his or her needs. Even very young children can express views about health issues (James, 1995; Ireland and Holloway, 1996).

Studies which ascertain the views of users, including children and young people, are important in pointing to aspects of service delivery that are valued by them and are particularly appropriate in determining quality standards. There is much experience from practice of services which were ineffective because too little account was taken of the users' perspectives – time schedules that suit professionals but not users; inappropriate venues; too little accounting of cultural norms; or failing to understand the user's needs – as reported earlier in respect of early years services (Birmingham, SSD, 1995) and in a review of ante- and post-natal education (Combes and Schonveld, 1992).

Existing examples of successful evaluation studies, whatever the methodology employed, tend to relate to relatively narrow social interventions. Testing the effectiveness of more complex initiatives, such as that depicted in Figure 9 on page 44, may require a different approach to evaluation. New ideas are emerging from America which offer an approach to evaluation that may be appropriate for comprehensive community initiatives (Connell and others, 1995; Connell and Kubisch, 1996). These authors propose a 'theory of change' framework, which is based on clearly articulated programme aims, developed interactively with all stakeholders and linked to ongoing assessment of activities and outcomes throughout the operation of the initiative. This framework, which has still to be tested in practice, appears to combine the benefits of rigorous experimental designs with those of more qualitative methods.

This discussion suggests that in developing a future research and development programme, it will be necessary to include studies with a range of research methodologies. As we have suggested elsewhere in relation specifically to evaluating parent education programmes (McGuire and Smith, 1996), providing evidence of the effectiveness of interventions will require a programme of research, with different types of study addressing different research questions and taking account of different perspectives on outcomes. Such a programme is likely to include experimental or quasi-experimental design studies such as random controlled trials, but these will be complemented by other methodologies more appropriate for process evaluations. It is important to demonstrate attribual outcomes from defined interventions. It is also important to understand why the outcome has occurred – the process issues. Part of this is enabling parents and children to express their views on the impact of a particular intervention, whether or how they think things have changed. Studies which ascertain the views of users – and non-users or those who dropout – using qualitative methods, are a valid part of evaluating an intervention. Did users feel they were treated with dignity and respect? Do they think that professionals listened, gave them the opportunity to participate and express their opinions? Why were some people not attracted to the services; or did not continue their involvement? Evidence gathered in this way is very necessary in establishing and assessing quality standards in work with families. It is often only by ensuring families have a platform that we can address their agendas, including the negatives, rather than those of service providers or researchers.

# 6.  A research and development agenda

This review of the contribution of mainstream services to preventive work has led us to ask many questions, which we now draw together. The questions raised and those still to be answered fall into four different sets:

- First, where there is insufficient knowledge about the causes or nature of child and families difficulties or ways of promoting the well-being of children. Here the research questions are about the origins and composition of those 'snakes and ladders' (see page 7) which beset children.
- Second, where it seems there is sufficient knowledge (either about risk and protective factors or about attributes of services) but this has not been translated into preventive work. Here the questions need to focus on barriers to the adoption or development of appropriate services.
- Third, where mainstream preventive services have been created but their impact has not been subject to objective review. The questions for evaluative research are about testing the impact or effectiveness of those social interventions, their sustainability, transferability and replicability.
- Fourth, where there is sufficient knowledge to suggest a particular intervention has potential in promoting the well-being of children. Here the emphasis shifts to a development agenda; to the development of a new service based on identified local needs or to adoption of new practice, both of which must be subject to rigorous evaluation.

Two other areas of activity are also required to complement this research and development programme:

- coordinated information collation and exchange on innovative preventive programmes and the results of any evaluation exercises on these;

- the need for a policy agenda to promote decision-making based on our existing knowledge and understanding.

In this report we can do no more than mark the significance of the first point. The second we consider briefly in our concluding remarks.

## Constructing a research and development agenda

The construction of this agenda takes account of and is bounded by the parameters established in Section 2. The research and development agenda set out below is grouped under the four headings noted above and abbreviated to knowledge, barriers, evaluation and development. While the distinction between these groups is useful we also recognise there will be significant over-laps. Similarly, the four themes discussed in Section 3 are best seen, as cross-cutting themes. These themes are:

- initiatives to support and enhance the parenting task;
- child health surveillance programmes;
- social service work with children;
- preventing 'anti-social' behaviour in adolescence.

It is not our intention to construct specific research questions nor to design development strategies. Our purpose is simply to construct a future agenda within these broad topic areas.

## Research and development agenda

### Knowledge

- Comparative studies are needed into the human and financial costs of supporting children in need and their families in different ways. Examples would include the delivery of family support through the school setting compared to an area social services office; use of outreach, though school based, support staff compared to education welfare officers; comparative effectiveness of early intervention through home visiting; the use of open access mental health services rather than clinically based filtered or referred access services.
- Improved understanding of the
  - acceptability and impact (particularly on the behaviour of both parents and children) of differently designed and delivered parenting education initiatives, including age

appropriateness, cultural relevance, attention to adult learning, the role of the extended family and social networks.

— parenting tasks and styles from the perspective of its 'customers', that is children and young people. This could include comparing the perspectives of parents and children and young people.

— the role of fathers in contemporary society as new parents, as fathers of young children and as parents of adolescents.

— the potential of young people to contribute constructively to the effective management and overall performance of schools, including the standards of discipline and behaviour and to exclusion and inclusion processes.

● Health promotion as a mainstream service may be able to improve its contribution to meeting the needs of particular groups of vulnerable families but we lack the knowledge to underpin an appropriate development strategy.

● We know insufficient about the gatekeeping of services and the impact that this has on access. We need to identify who the key gatekeepers are in health, education, housing, leisure, and social care and determine whether they are sufficiently informed to act in this role, how they use the information they have and what could help improve their role.

## Barriers

● The majority of people with 'greatest needs' resulting from circumstances such as poverty, learning difficulties or poor parenting experiences do not readily access mainstream provision. We need to understand the barriers to access and/or acceptance of services by such families in a range of fields including child health advice, parenting skills and social work services.

● Barriers such as language, public image, organisational culture, job descriptions and myths appear to prevent collaborative interventions occurring between agencies with common target groups. We need more understanding of how these barriers operate and how they can be overcome when delivering services such as those for young people with mental health problems, emotional and behavioural difficulties or those children excluded from school.

- An analysis is required of the factors which promote or prevent community based practices becoming a mainstream intervention. Work in this area would include users' perceptions of mainstream services; policing versus support activity and the attitudes and skill base of the relevant professions for the task.
- Where research tells us that certain services would be of benefit to young people but practice shows they do not use them, we need to find out why. This may include drug advise and education, youth clubs, health advice centres and after school clubs.

## Evaluation

- The role and potential of youth workers, community outreach workers, including those employed to work within specific minority ethnic communities, and community leaders, to meet the needs of troubled young people as against all young people should be evaluated.
- Similarly the role of health visitors is changing from a universal response service to targeting vulnerable families. This may have a positive or negative effect or no impact at all on 'outcomes' such as prevention of family breakdown, parenting problems and access to resources.
- Legislation which affects children can have the effect of changing the way mainstream services are delivered without due attention to the impact of the changes upon children. We need a continuous programme evaluating the impact of existing and new legislation which affects children and young people. This would include health, social welfare, transport, education and environmental legislation.
- More systematic and independent evaluation is required of the impact of services that appear to be valued by and effective for their users, such as integrated early years centres, open access family centres, adolescent resource centres and youth drop-in centres.

## Development

- Development work within schools is needed to improve a school's ability to engage parents and to ensure their participation beyond the traditional fundraising and parents' evening activities. This is particularly so with parents who have difficulties with parenting, authority and the educational process. This may include the dissemination of existing good practice as well as the support of schools to examine their role.

- Work in localities within the mainstream environments for men as the route to engaging them in enhancing their role as parents. This may include establishing development initiatives with local services to achieve changes which are transferable elsewhere, for example through local football clubs.

- Work across agency boundaries with school based health staff and health trusts as providers of health expertise to vulnerable children and families in an education setting is needed.

- Work is needed to show how the use of residential care as a preventive intervention within a continuum of care in neighbourhoods can be put into practice. (Sect 20 Children Act.)

- Work is required to translate into practice conceptual models of preventive work such as those proposed by Utting and others, 1993; Farrington, 1996; Hearn, 1995 and Rea Price and Pugh, 1995; the Audit Commission, 1996; and as elsewhere, for evaluation of both process and outcomes to be built in.

- The development of a framework to support the dissemination of innovative pieces of work found to be effective in one area to other areas, through an independent medium, in order to increase their chances of broader adoption.

- The current 'refocusing of practice' debate requires development work targeted at first level managers and practitioners from health, social care and education settings. By working together it would be possible to develop practice that is locally relevant and uses collective and community resources to improve the outcomes for families and children in need.

## A priority research and development agenda

The agenda we have constructed is of necessity both long and broad. From that we have selected five priority areas.

- *Earlier we identified a number of conceptual models of preventative work, some deduced from research evidence, some from practice experience and others a mix of the two. Can these be translated into practice and with identifiable outcomes for children and families?*

  In this context we would suggest a major comparative study of the effectiveness – the balance between the human and financial costs and the outcomes for children and families – of delivering family support through three different settings – a school, an area social services office and a health centre.

- *What are the channels across and the barriers between voluntary and / or community led initiatives and mainstream statutory services and who are the gatekeepers that open the channels or sustain the barriers?*

  In particular we suggest these issues could be illustrated with a study which focuses on the role of voluntary or community provision in supporting parents with mental health problems and their children; how do they and how might they act as a channel to specialist mental health services for these families in need? Similarly, coming in the other direction, are GPs and other professional groups sufficiently informed about community based initiatives to be able to access these for their patients to complement or replace more specialist health provision?

- *How do children and young people perceive and understand particular aspects of their social world and their contribution to it?*

  Here we identify as important children's perception of parenting. What do children and young people see as the task of parenting; what do they expect and what do they think they get from their parents; how does this differ between fathers and others; who else do they see as contributing to their 'parenting'; how do children and young people characterise different parenting styles; which do they like most and which do they see as most effective?

  By talking with diverse groups of young people across ethnic, class and ability clusters it would be possible to ensure that their views are used to inform the development of parenting education and skills enhancement – applicable to the parenting of both young children and adolescents.

- *What motivates or discourages people in 'greatest need' to seek help from their family; from social networks / friendship groups; from their local / ethnic community; from voluntary agencies; or from statutory providers.*

  Why might some potential sources of help be chosen and not others? How or where do these families gather their intelligence about where to gain assistance? What factors might influence this? What attributes encourage or support those in 'greatest need' seeking help – for instance easy access, non-stigmatising, empowering? What frustrates attempts at gaining help?

We recommend two areas where we think these questions are particularly relevant; the uptake by families in 'greatest need' of child health advice and the uptake of parenting education.

- *How can men be guided and supported in their parenting role particularly with adolescent male children?*

What services or supports currently exist for fathers? How helpful are they? How should they be supplemented? New service developments might be directed at engaging men through existing social systems such as local sports or social clubs, football clubs, the workplace; using employers, high profile clubs and any others to promote the value and necessity of fathering to men.

As with all proposals for new developments, this must include monitoring and evaluation of the outcomes achieved.

# 7.   Outlining a policy agenda

So what contribution can mainstream services make to preventive work? As is evident from the text the answer is not a simple one. Rather than repeat the arguments presented earlier we will summarise key points which arise and offer the outline of a policy agenda. Hopefully readers will see these as important issues which they can develop, promote and most importantly of all play their part in taking forward.

## A prevention strategy
To make this review manageable we have chosen four different themes reflecting a range of family concerns. We are aware that is this not comprehensive, nor can these four themes be treated in isolation. There are identified links between child health promotion, family support, school achievement, and young people's behaviour. Yet preventive or early intervention initiatives appear fragmented – a parenting programme here, a mental health drop-in centre there – often with insecure funding and isolated from more mainstream provision.

How then do we deliver family support initiatives which are acceptable to families, are cost effective and which make sense in terms of a preventive strategy which is delivered through mainstream services? This is the overarching policy question raised by this review. To address this we suggest a policy agenda with six main items, which are introduced below.

## Balancing universal and targeted services
We have identified that preventive services have a part to play at all levels – preventing the onset of problems, preventing simple problems from magnifying and preventing the worst effects of serious difficulties. To do this they need to focus on universal

needs, on community needs and on specific child or family needs. Universal services must be the basis of a preventive strategy, but on their own they are not sufficient. Some families require a deeper and more substantial investment. So universal or open access services must be able to provide a channel, in a way that is non-stigmatising, to more specialist services.

It is also important that the right match is made between needs and services at each level. Even services that are open to all must have a clear focus in terms of what they aim to achieve. This requires careful needs assessment at a community and individual level, with services targeted where they can have most impact. Assessment of need must be complemented by an assessment of risk, including the risk which arises from **not** providing support. This will give a more complete picture of 'costs' to inform resource allocations.

### Reassessing resource priorities

While accepting the adage 'better at fence at the top of the cliff than an ambulance at the bottom', at times of budget contraction it may seem more immediately cost effective to maintain ever ageing ambulances than to switch resources to the construction of a well designed fence at the top of the cliff. This is even more so when the ageing ambulance is seen as a 'statutory' requirement, but the fence is an 'optional' extra. The Audit Commission (1996) in its report *Misspent Youth* demonstrates clearly that this is not the case – spending resources on processing the outcomes of problem behaviour rather than preventing it is, in their view, inefficient and ineffective. Nonetheless, today there are many who believe that sustained budget cuts in mainstream statutory services means that funding barely covers the ambulances which assist those that fall let alone construct any fences. Developing preventive services is going to require a reassessment of resource priorities at central and local government levels.

### Sustaining professional motivation

Reallocating priorities in resource allocation and service delivery needs staff with vitality, vision and energy. All of these attributes can be drained when mainstream services are under pressure – when class size expands, when the youth service is squeezed, when referrals to social services continue to grow and the ratio of health visitors, school nurses and education welfare officers to children increases. How then are we to motivate staff, who are over pressurised and whose professional self-esteem is at a low ebb, to draw breath and to put the necessary energy into refocusing their practice – to develop services and methods of working which are characterised by the attributes, the seven A's, described in Section 4?

Not only may professionals need to be encouraged to keep going, they need to be supported to move on. The implementation of a preventive strategy may require new professional demarcations of tasks and roles. We need to know more about which professionals and which skills are best fitted to deliver which services in a more collaborative world serving a preventive agenda. This is likely to require more than new job descriptions; equally important is the need to redesign training to ensure cross disciplinary staff development that promotes the understanding that each profession has of others. Joint, multi-disciplinary training of staff, both initial and in-service training, is essential if the barriers to working effectively across traditional agency boundaries are to be broken down.

### Children's Services Plans

Currently we have an array of small, medium and large services, from all sectors, charged with the task of supporting children and their families. How do we ensure that all these cohere and together ensure that the fence is a solid construction without too many gaps or overlaps?

Children's Services Plans offer a framework for a cross sector, cross agency strategic plan based on assessment of the many dimensions of the needs of children and their families – health, educational, environmental, transport, housing, welfare, and informed by the views of those needing services. Auditing current services and matching against needs should identify gaps and instigate a planning process that indicates the appropriate balance between mainstream and specialist services and effectively link one to the other.

But Children's Services Plans must be more than a paper exercise; as a strategic planning tool for **all** children they must demand an active response, and where appropriate bring about a realignment in professional priorities and service provision.

### New multi-agency structures

A collective preventive strategy will need new organisational structures that require people to work together across agencies. A first step towards this may be joint or shared commissioning by local agencies. A comprehensive family based model of preventive activity, as described in the report, will require substantial investment – either of new money or a redistribution of existing resources – and collaboration from all agencies in all sectors. Central government needs to take a lead in demonstrating collaboration and communication through coherent legislation and policies which are internally consistent and which promotes locally delivered agendas for action on prevention.

Ultimately it may be necessary to review the span of operational control of public officials to ensure that it is bounded in a way that allows objectives to be tackled with the right combination of resources. This may go beyond the current understanding of Children's Services Planning to a more fundamental restructuring of children's services across all sectors and services.

New service developments need to be designed to promote those identified attributes of effective services – the seven A's discussed in Section 4. Particular emphasis needs to be given to listening to children, young people and families, consulting with them and actively involving them in the planning and delivery of services.

### Sharing information, monitoring outcomes

Implementing a broad based preventive programme of family support is predicated upon coherent locality planning. Linking provision, storing, updating and accessing detailed information on services requires that cross agency resources are used to create an over arching system of information. Not only is this necessary for coordination, it is vital for families, to facilitate their access to services. The technology is available for such information sharing, but the will to invest is still lacking.

Information systems are also needed to measure performance towards achieving the goals set by a preventive strategy. Choosing the appropriate performance and outcomes measures may be problematic, but nonetheless is an essential part of any family intervention.

The policy agenda outlined above has implications for all levels of government – central government, local authorities, health agencies, area or locality teams in local communities. Developing and implementing a preventive strategy to promote the well-being of all children and their families will not be achieved overnight. It requires long term planning. That in turn requires vision and commitment. The future well-being of our society demands nothing less.

# References

Aldgate, J and Tunstill, J (1995) *Making Sense of Section 17. Implementing Services for Children in Need Within the 1989 Children Act.* HMSO

Aplin, G and Pugh, G (1983) *Perspectives on Preschool Home Visiting.* National Children's Bureau

Aye Maung, N (1995) *Young People, Victimisation and the Police: British crime survey findings on experiences and attitudes of 12 to 15-year-olds.* HMSO

Audit Commission (1994) *Seen But Not Heard: Coordinating community child health and social services for children in need.* HMSO

Audit Commission (1996) *Misspent Youth: Young people and crime.* Audit Commission Publications

Barclay, P (1982) *Social Workers: Their role and tasks.* (The Barclay Report) National Institute for Social Work

Barker, C (1996) *Nowhere to Hide: Giving young runaways a voice.* Centrepoint in partnership with NSPCC

Barker, W, Anderson, R and Chambers, C (1992) *Child Protection: The impact of the child development programme.* Department of Social Work, Bristol University

Barn, R, Sinclair, R and Ferdinand, D (1997) *Acting on Principle Race and Ethnicity in Social Service Provision to Children and Families.* BAAF

Bastiani, J and Wolfendale, S (1996) *Home-School Work in Britain: Review, reflection and development.* David Fulton

Bavolek, S (1990) 'Parenting: theory, policy and practice', *Research and Validation Report of the Nurturing Programmes.* US, Winconsin: Eau Claire, Family Development Resources Inc.

Berrueta-Clement, J and others (1984) *Changed Lives. The Effects of the Perry Pre-School Programme on Youths Through Age 19.* US, Michigan: High Scope Press

Birmingham City Council. Social Services Department (1996) *The Wraparound Project Final Report.* Birmingham City Council

Blackburn, C (1991) *Parenting and Health: Working with families.* Open University

Blyth, E and Milner, J (1993) 'Exclusion from school: A first step in exclusion from society?' *Children and Society,* 7, 3, 255–68

Bradley, C and Road, F (1994) *A Team Approach to Meeting Special Educational Needs.* Oxfordshire Special Needs Research Project. Oxford

Bradshaw, J (1990) *Child Poverty and Deprivation in the UK*. National Children's Bureau

Bryant, G (1986) 'Preventive health care for pre-school children or health surveillance', *Child Care, Health and Development*, 12, 195–206

Buchanan, A, Wheal, A and Barlow, J (1995) *How to Stay out of Trouble: Views of young young people who have offended in Wiltshire*. Barnardo's

Bunyan, A and Sinclair, R (1987) 'Gatekeepers to care', *Practice*, 2, 116–128 (PARA 2)

Burgess, A and Ruxton, S (1996) *Men and Their Children: Proposals for public policy*. Institute for Public Policy Research

Burghes, L (1994) *Lone Parenthood and Family Disruption: The outcomes for children*. Family Policy Studies Unit

Butler, J (1989) *Child Health Surveillance in Primary Care: A critical review*. HMSO

Cannan, C (1992) *Changing Families, Changing Welfare: Family centres and the welfare state*. Harvester Wheatsheaf

Centre for the Study of Social Policy (1990) *Helping Families Grow Strong. New Directions in Public Policy*. Papers from the colloquium on public policy and family support. US

Cochrane Collaboration (1994) *Guidelines for assessing methodological quality*. Cochrane Centre

Combes, G and Schonveld, A (1992) *Life Will Never Be the Same Again: Learning to be a first-time Parent. A review of antenatal and postnatal health education*. Health Education Authority

Committee of Enquiry into Discipline in Schools (1989) *Discipline in Schools : Report of the committee of enquiry chaired by Lord Elton*. Department of Education and Science/Welsh Office

Connell, J and Kubisch, A C (1996) *Applying a Theories of Change Approach to the Evaluation of Comprehensive Community Initiatives: Progress, prospects and problems*. (Unpublished Draft)

Connell, J and others (1995) *New Approaches to Evaluating Community Initiatives: Concepts, methods, and contexts*. US. Washington: The Aspen Institute

Coohey, C and Marsh, J (1995) 'Promotion, prevention and treatment: what are the differences?', *Research in Social Work Practice*, 5(4), 524–538

Coopers & Lybrand (1994) *Preventive Strategy for Young People in Trouble*. Coopers & Lybrand

Cowan, C P (1988) 'Working with men becoming fathers: the impact of a couples group intervention'*in* Bronstein P and Cowan C P *Fatherhood Today: Men's Changing Role in the Family*. Wiley

Department of Education and Science (1972) *Education: A framework for expansion*. White Paper Cmnd 5174

Department of Education and Science (1989) *Discipline in schools: Report of the Committee of Enquiry (Elton Report)* HMSO

Department for Education and Employment (1995) *Grants for Education Support and Training (GEST) Scheme: Truancy and disaffected pupils category. Directory of approved projects 1994–95*. Department for Education and Employment

Department of Health and Department of Education (1995) *A Handbook on Child and Adolescent Mental Health*. HMSO

Department of Health and Department for Education and Employment (1996)

*Children's Services Planning: Guidance.* The Department of Health and Department for Education and Employment

Department of Health. Social Services Inspectorate (1995) *Children's Services Plans: An analysis of children's services plans 1993/94.* Department of Health

Department of Health (1991) *Patterns and Outcomes in Child Placement: Messages from current research and their implications.* HMSO

Department of Health (1994) *Child Welfare and the Appropriate Role of Family Support within Child Protection Services.* (Sieff Conference)

Department of Health (1995) *Child Protection Messages from Research.* HMSO

Department of Health and Social Security (1974a) *The Family in Society: Dimensions of parenthood.* HMSO

Department of Health and Social Security (1974b) *The Family in Society: Preparation for parenthood.* HMSO

Department of Health and Social Security (1985) *Social Work Decisions in Child Care: Recent research findings and their implications.* HMSO

Dunne-Maxim, K and others (1992) 'The aftermath of youth suicide: providing postvention services for the school and community', *Crisis,* 13, 1, 16–22

Elfer, P and Gatis, S (1990) *Charting Child Health Services: A survey of community child health services provided by health authorities in England, Scotland and Wales.* National Children's Bureau

Farrington, D (1996) *Understanding and Preventing Youth Crime.* Joseph Rowntree Foundation

Farrington, D and West, D (1982) *Delinquency: Its roots, careers and prospects.* Heinemann

Ferri, E and Saunders, A (1991) *Parents, Professionals and Pre-School Centres: A study of Barnardo's provision.* National Children's Bureau

Fischer, J (1976) *The Effectiveness of Social Casework.* Springfield Il: Charles C Thomas

Fischer, J (1973) 'Is casework effective: a review'. *Social Work,* 17, 1–5

Freeman, R (1992) 'The idea of prevention: a critical review' *in* Scott, S, Williams, G, Platt, S and Thomas, H *eds.* (1992) *Private Risks and Public Dangers: Explorations in Sociology.* Avebury

Frost, N (1996) *Negotiated Friendship: Home-Start and the delivery of family support.* University of Leeds

Fuller, R (1987) *Researching Prevention: A research note.* University of Stirling Social Work Research Centre

Gardner, R (1992) *Supporting Families: Preventive social work in practice.* National Children's Bureau

Gibbons, J and Thorpe, S (1989) 'Can voluntary support projects help vulnerable families? The work of Home-Start', *British Journal of Social Work,* 19, 189–202

Gibbons, J (1989) *Purpose and Organisation of Preventive Work with Families: The two area study.* Department of Health

Gibbons, J, Thorpe, S, and Wilkinson, P (1990) *Family Support and Prevention.* National Institute for Social Work. HMSO

Gibbons, J, Conroy, S and Bell, C (1995) *Operating the Child Protection System: A study of child protection practices in English Local Authorities.* HMSO

Graham, J (1988) *Schools Disruptive Behaviour.* HMSO

Graham, J and Bowling, B (1995) *Young People and Crime.* Home Office

Guba, E and Lincoln, V (1989) *Fourth Generation Evaluation.* Sage Publications

Hagell, A and Newburn, T (1994a) *Persistent Young Offenders.* Policy Studies Institute

Hagell, A and Newburn, T (1994b) *Young Offenders and the Media: Viewing habits and preferences.* Policy Studies Institute

Hall, D (ed) (1989, 1991, 1996) *Health For All Children.* Oxford University Press.

Hardiker, P, Exton, K and Barker, M (1991a) *Policies and Practices in Preventive Child Care.* Avebury/Gower

Hardiker, P, Exton K and Barker, M (1991b) 'The Social Policy Contexts of Prevention in Child Care', *British Journal of Social Work,* 21, 4, 341–359

Harman, D and Brim, O (1980) *Learning to be a Parent: Principles and methods.* Sage Publications

Hayden, L (1994) 'Primary age children excluded from school: A multi agency focus for concern'. *Children & Society,* 8, 3, 257–73

Hearn, B (1995) *Child and Family Support and Protection: A practical approach.* National Children's Bureau

Hodgkin, R and Newell, P (1996) *Effective Government Structures for Children.* Guilbenkian Foundation

Hohmamm, M, Bannet, B and Weikart, D (1976) *Young Children in Action.* High/Scope Press

Holman, R (1980) *Inequality in Child Care.* Child Poverty Action Group

Holman, R (1988) *Putting Families First: Prevention and child care.* Children's Society/Macmillan

Holtermann, S (1995a) *Investing in Young Children: Reassessing the cost on education and day care services.* National Children's Bureau

Holtermann, S (1995b) *All Our Futures: The impact of public expenditure and fiscal policies on Britain's children and young people.* Barnardo's

Home Office (1995) *Criminal Statistics.* HMSO

Inglis, S (1995) *Take Ten Families: Parents' experience of problems and sources of help in Scotland.* Children in Scotland

Ireland, L and Holloway, I (1996) 'Qualitative health research with children' *Children and Society,* 10, 2, 155–164

James, J (1995) 'Children speak about health'. *Primary Health Care,* 5, 10, 8–12

Johnson, Z and Molloy, B (1995) 'The community mothers programme – empowerment of parents by parents,' *Children and Society,* 9, 2, 73–83

Kempson, E (1996) *Life on a Low Income.* Joseph Rowntree Foundation. York Publishing Services

Kinder, K, Wakefield, A and Wilkin, A (1996) *Talking Back: Pupil views on disaffection.* NFER

Kumar, V (1993) *Poverty and Inequality in the UK: The effects on children.* National Children's Bureau

Kurtz, Z (1996) *Treating Children Well: A guide housing the evidence base in commissioning and managing services for the mental health of children and young people.* Mental Health Foundation

Larner, M and others (1992) *Fair Start for Children. Lessons learned from seven demonstration projects.* Yale University Press

Leach, P (1994) *Children First: What our society must do – is not doing – for our children today.* Michael Joseph

Learmonth, J (1995) *More Willingly to School? An independent evaluation of the truancy and disaffected pupils GEST programme.* Department for Education and Employment

Lewis, E (1996) 'Truancy – the partnership approach'. *Young People Now*, 85, 32–33

Lloyd, C (1994) *The Welfare Net: How well does the net work?* Oxford Brookes University.

MacDonald, A, Sheldon, B and Gillespie, J (1992) 'Contemporary studies of the effectiveness of social work', *British Journal of Social*, 22, 6, 615–643

Macdonald, G and Roberts, H (1995) *What Works in the Early Years? Effective interventions for children and their families in health, social welfare, education and child protection.* Barnardo's

Macfarlane, J and Pillnay, U (1984) 'Who does what, and how much in the preschool child health services in England'. *British Medical Journal*, 289, 851–2

McGuire C and Smith, C (1996) *Evaluating Parent Education Programmes: Paper presented to Joseph Rowntree Foundation.*

McQuail, S and Pugh, G (1995) *Effective Organisation of Early Childhood Services.* National Children's Bureau

Makins, V (1997) *The Invisible Children: Nipping failure in the bud.* The National Pyramid Trust

Malek, M (1996) *Making Home-School Work: Home-School Work and the East London Schools Fund.* National Children's Bureau

Malek, M (1997) *Nurturing Healthy Minds: Voluntary sector initiatives promoting children's mental health.* National Children's Bureau

Mayall, B (1986) *Keeping Children Healthy.* Allen and Unwin

Medway, F (1989) 'Assessing the effectiveness of parent education' *in* Fine, M (ed) *The Second Handbook of Parent Education.* Academic Press

NHS Health Advisory Service (1995) *Child Adolescent Mental Health Services: Together we stand. Commissioning, role and management of child and adolescent mental health services.* HMSO

Nuffield Health Unit (1996) 'Preventing unintentional injuries in children and young adolescents', *Effective Health Care*, 2, 5

Oakley, A and others (1995) *Sexual Health Education Interactions for Young People.* British Medical Journal, 310, 6973, 158–162

Oakley, A and Roberts, H, eds. (1996) *Evaluating Social Interventions.* Barnardo's

Ofsted (1996) *Exclusions from Secondary Schools.* The Stationery Office

Oppenheim, C.A and Harper, L (1996) *Poverty: The facts.* Child Poverty Action Group

Packman, J, Randall, J and Jacques, N (1986) *Who Needs Care? Social Work Decisions about Children.* Blackwell

Packman, J and Jordan, B (1991) 'The Children Act: Looking forward, looking back'. *British Journal of Social Work*, 21, 4

Parker, H & Sutherland, H (1991) *Child Tax allowances? A comparison of child benefit, child tax reliefs and basic incomes as instruments of family policy.* STICERD Occasional Paper No.16. London School of Economics

Parker, R (ed.) and others (1991) *Looking After Children: Assessing outcomes in child care.* HMSO

Parsons, C (1996) 'Permanent exclusions from schools in England and Wales in the 1990s: trends, causes and responses'. *Children and Society*, 10, 3, 177–186

Parton, N (1996) 'Child protection, family support and social work: A critical appraisal of the Department of Health research studies in child protection'. *Child and Family Social Work*, 1, 1, 3–11

Parton, N (1985) *The Politics of Child Abuse*. Macmillan

Patterson, G.R (1982) *Coercive Family Process*. US. Eugene, Oregon: Castalia

Patterson, G and Narrett, C (1990) 'The development of a reliable and valid treatment programme for aggressive young children'. *International Journal of Mental Health*, 19, 3, 19–26

Pitts, J and Smith, P (1995) *Preventing School Bullying*. Crime Prevention and Detection Series No.63. Police Research Group: Home Office

Pugh, G and De'Ath E (1989) *Working Towards Partnership in the Early Years*. National Children's Bureau

Pugh, G, De'Ath, E and Smith, C (1994) *Confident Parents, Confident Children: Policy and practice in parent education and support*. National Children's Bureau

Pugh, G and De'Ath, E (1984) *The Needs of Parents*. National Children's Bureau

Rea Price, J and Pugh, G (1995) *Championing Children: A report on Manchester City Council's services for children*. National Children's Bureau

Reid, W and Hanrahan, P (1980) 'The effectiveness of social work: recent evidence'. Goldberg and Connelly (eds) *The Effectiveness of Social Care for the Elderly*. Heinemann

Richards, M (1994) *The Interests of Children at Divorce*. (Paper presented to the 'Families and Justice' international conference, Brussels)

Roberts, C (1995) *A National Study of Parents and Parenting Problems*. Family Policy Studies Centre

Robins, D (1990) *Sport as Prevention. The role of sport in crime prevention programmes aimed at young people*. University of Oxford: Centre for Criminological Research

Rutter, M (1974) 'Dimensions of parenthood: some myths and some suggestions' in *The Family in Society: dimensions of parenthood*, Department of Health and Social Security, HMSO

Rutter, M (1985) 'Resilience in the Face of Adversity: protective factors and resistance to psychiatric disorder'. *British Journal of Psychiatry*, 147, pp. 598–611

Rutter, M and Madge, N (1976) *Cycles of disadvantage*. Heinmann

Rutter, M and Smith, D (1995) *Psychosocial Disorders in Young People: Time trends and their causes*. Wiley

Sammons, P, Hillman, J and Mortimore, P (1995) *Key Characteristics of Effective Schools: A review of school effectiveness research*. OFSTED

Schaffer, R (1990) *Making Decisions About Children*. Blackwell

Schweinhert, L, Barnes, H V and Weikart, D P (1993) *Significant Benefits: The High / Scope Perry Pre-School Study through age 27*. US: Michigan. High/Scope Press

Sheldon, B (1986) 'Social work effectiveness experiments: review and implications'. *British Journal of Social Work*', 16, 223–242

Shinman, S (1981) *A Chance for Every Child: Access and response to pre-school provision*. Tavistock Publications

Shucksmith, J, Hendry, L, and Glendinning, A (1995) 'Models of parenting: implications for adolescent well being within different types of family contexts'. *Journal of Adolescence*, 18, 3, 253–70

Slavin, R (1992) 'Preventing early school failure: what works?'. *Educational Leadership*. December, 237pp

Smale, G (1989) *Pictures of Practice: vol 1 – Community Social Work in Scotland*. National Institute for Social Work

Smale, G (1990) *Pictures of Practice: vol 2 – Partners in Empowerment: Networks of innovation in social work*. National Institute for Social Work

Smale, G (1992) *Managing Change Through Innovation*. National Institute for Social Work

Smith, C and Pugh, G (1996) *Learning to be a Parent: a survey of group-based parenting programmes*. Joseph Rowntree Foundation and National Children's Bureau Enterprises

Smith, C (1996) *Developing parenting programmes*. Joseph Rowntree Foundation and National Children's Bureau Enterprises

Statham, J (1994) *Childcare in the Community*. Save the Children Fund

Stein and Gambrill, (1977) 'Facilitating decision making in foster care', *Social Services Review*, 51, 502–511

Sutton, J, Jagger, C, and Smith, L.K (1995) 'Parents' views of health surveillance'. *Archives of Disease in Childhood*, 73, 1, 57–61

Sutton, P (1995) *Crossing the Boundaries: A discussion of children's services plans*. National Children's Bureau

Sylva, K (1994) 'The impact of early leaving on children's later development' *in* Ball, C (1994) *Start Right: The importance of early learning*. Royal Society for the Encouragement of Arts, Manufactures and Commerce.

Thorpe, D (1988) 'Career patterns in child care – implications for service'. *British Journal of Social Work*. 18, 2, 137–153

Utting, D (1991) *Reducing Criminality Among Young People. A sample of relevant programmes in the UK*. Home Office Research Study 161

Utting, D (1995) *Family and Parenthood: Supporting families, preventing breakdown*. Joseph Rowntree Foundation

Utting, D, Bright, J and Henricson, C (1993) *Crime and the Family: improving child-rearing and preventing delinquency*. Family Policy Studies Centre

Van der Eyken, W (1982) *Home-Start: A four year evaluation*. Home-Start Consultancy

Whalley, M (1996) 'Partnerships with parents'. *Early Education*, 18, 6–8

Whalley, M (1994) *Learning to be Strong: Setting up a neighbourhood service for under fives and their families*. Hodder & Stoughton

Williamson, L (1995) 'Persecuted at home: destitute in the UK' *Childright*, no.122(Dec), pp8–10

Willow, C (1996) *Childrens Rights and Participation in Residential Care*. National Children's Bureau

Wilson, H (1987) 'Parental supervision re-examined', *British Journal of Criminology*, 20, 3, 203–235

Woodhead, C (1995) *A Question of Standards: Finding the balance*. Politeia

Woodhead, M (1985) 'Pre-school education has long-term effects: but can they be generalised? *Oxford Review of Education*, 11, 133–55

Woodhead, M (1996) *In Search of the Rainbow. Pathways to quality in large-scale programmes for young disadvantaged children*. The Netherlands: The Hague, Bernard Van Leer Foundation

# Index